LIFE IS WHAT YOU MAKE IT

Joyce Chatwin

RIVERHEAD

Joyce Chatwin

First published in Great Britain in 2019 by Riverhead

A CIP catalogue record for this book is
available from the British Library

ISBN 978-1-9164294-???

Design and Production by Riverhead
Kardomah 94,
94 Alfred Gelder Street, Hull HU1 2AN
Telephone: 07890 170063
email: mike.riverheadbooks@gmail.com

Printed by: Fisk Printing, Hull

LIFE IS WHAT YOU MAKE IT

CONTENTS

Joyce Chatwin

ACKNOWLEDGEMENTS

For my late husband Kenneth and for my children, Jenny Lyn, Kenneth, William and Mark who have given me their support for the whole of the last two years while I wrote this book and who brighten my life.

My special thanks go to my son Bill, who without his aid as editor, researcher and photographic restorer, this book could not have been written and published.

PREFACE

A short time after my father died in January 2014 and while helping my mother, with my brothers and sister, to sort through some belongings, I came across an old, worn red leather case. My mother was quite reluctant to let me open it but intrigued, I persisted and she eventually relented. Inside I found a number of notebooks, scraps of paper and pages torn from various writing pads. All were filled with my mother's handwriting and underneath laid a very old photo album.

It didn't take long for me to realise that the writings were related to the photographs in the album and were all about our family history. Some of the early photographs were obviously very old and judging by the clothes and context, within which they were set, dated back to the late 1800s.

The separate notebooks and pieces of paper contained anecdotes, which had obviously been triggered by many of the photographs and my mother, after a lot of persuasion let me read through her accounts of lives and events from the end of the 19th Century up until the new millennium, while protesting that she was embarrassed because she couldn't write well.

Trying to ignore her protests I knew that I had in my hands something special. It was special for two reasons. Firstly the collector of these photographs and composer of the photograph album, my Great Grandmother, Jane Forth, must have realised how important photographs were going to become, as a way of recording the history of the families to follow and events of importance to social history, both local to the fishing community of Hull and to wider national and world events. Secondly, my mother had spent much of her early childhood very close to her Grandmother Jane, listening to stories about life and our predecessors from a time long before she was born.

My mother had the presence of mind and apparently urged on

by my father, to begin to write down the stories that she had heard from my Great Grandmother and other relatives and then her stories from her own life experiences. **(EDIT?)**

Unfortunately my mother was too modest to realise her own writing capabilities, often put down in a colloquial style, giving them authenticity and honesty that do justice to the images from the album. She had been writing for a number of years but always in secret or perhaps in private, as she wasn't really sure what she would eventually do with them.

I, along with my brothers and sister, realised just how important the words and photographs would be to our extended family, to Hull and East Yorkshire and possibly to some with a wider and more academic interest and after some persistent persuasion, mother relented and let me transpose all of her words to the computer and digitise and restore the photographs.

We began to realise that this 'project' had the makings of something more than just a private family history and as well as the possibilities of a self produced, self printed, family history, there might be something more to be made from this combination of words and images. So, over the best part of three years, my mother has continued to write, often filling out rough drafts from her notebooks but also expanding the stories that lay within the red case. As my mother became bolder and more confident, she talked to members of the family to, 'sharpen' some of her more blurry memories and with the wonders of technology, reference books and more traditional sources such as The Hull History Centre, I helped to research and confirm many of the details that came from my mother's remarkable memory.

I took on the role of adviser and editor and with many phone calls from Leeds, where I have lived since the seventies, back to Cherry Burton, where my mother now lives, and many trips up and down the M62 for face-to-face discussions we have worked on what you now hold in your hands.

I have thoroughly enjoyed the experience and feel so proud to have been a part of the process that was started and completed by these two remarkable women and has now become a legacy for our family and for posterity.

Bill Chatwin

INTRODUCTION

Writing about oneself is not easy. Having spent most of my life with my family, before and during marriage, I felt compelled to leave something of myself for my offspring.

You will appreciate that much of this story will be known to you but read on to uncover the unknown - and remember, I DID IT MY WAY.

So here goes, for you, my family and my grandchildren and great grandchildren.

For many years I have wanted to write these stories, having been very close to my Grandmother Jane and immersed in the true stories you have yet to read.

My Grandma Jane told me her life stories and much more. Being her only granddaughter I spent many hours being taught cooking, preparing food, gardening, sewing with a machine, knitting and even mending and re-soling shoes and boots. Another lesson learned was how to manage money through good housekeeping.

She also left me a rather old, battered photograph album. To me a most precious item. Some of the photographs go way back to Victorian times and all depict ancestors - and all the ancestors have their stories.

So with the aid of The Album I shall endeavour to share life as Grandma Jane (Forth) knew it and as I know it up to the present day.

Jane Forth
(born 1874 in the Drypool
District of Hull)

Jane's parents, Mr and Mrs Baker

PART 1

The First Generation
JANE FORTH
(nee Baker)

The first photograph in the album shows Jane's parents, Mr and Mrs Baker, standing in front of a house on Holderness Road. Mr Baker, Jane's father, worked at the Gas Works in Hull. They also had a son, brother to Jane, who joined the Royal Navy, and later joined the ranks of the very early submariners. William Baker was his name but he unfortunately lost his life serving his country, leaving behind a widow with two children, a girl and a boy. The boy, called Billy, was later photographed wearing a child's naval style uniform and his father's medal. Also in the album we see Mr Baker photographed with his daughter-in-law, in widow's weeds with the two children.

Jane's early years were spent at her Grandmother's house, somewhere in Holderness. She loved being outdoors roaming about collecting the eggs from beneath the chickens etc. She also had the company of her uncles and their many musical instruments of which she was to mention, many times. They included concertinas, penny whistles and tambourines. I was never to know the connection with music but I do know that the love of music was to continue through our family.

As time went on there came a day when Jane was to return home, she was needed as her father was now at home suffering with problems with his legs and as was the case at that time, he was receiving very little, if any financial support. This was, unfortunately, the beginning of a change in lifestyle for

Mr Baker with his daughter-in-law and her two children

LIFE IS WHAT YOU MAKE IT

Grandma. She found that she had to help to support her parents somehow. Jane was twelve years old and was sent to housekeep for a lady who was confined to bed with a new-born baby and other children in the family. She told me that everything went well for a while until she noticed that the husband was taking too much of an interest in her. Her parents told her to leave, so Jane went on to have many cleaning jobs.

As time passed she began to blossom so to speak. She found work keeping house for a publican's wife, which she enjoyed. One day the publican shouted through from the bar for Jane to come through and help with some clean glasses and this was the beginning of Jane meeting the customers. Being all male, Jane said that she felt a bit embarrassed, keeping her eyes down, cleaning glasses, pretending to ignore the whistles and remarks that she could hear and trying not to smile. This extra work gradually began to happen more regularly until she was offered more hours behind the bar. She gradually became accustomed to the banter and all the smiling faces. One evening there was something of a stir in the pub as someone opened the door to tell the crowd that, 'Bill's coming tonight, he landed today'. The majority of these men were fishermen, landing their catches at the now famous St Andrews Fish Dock in Hull. The call, 'Bill's home', caused quite a buzz. One of the customers at the bar asked for a pint for Bill, and still mystified, Jane asked, "Who is this Bill?"

The answer was, "Oh Bill's a laugh, and you'll like him. He'll be in tonight and you'll be kept busy at the pumps."

She soon found out who Bill was. As he came through the door, the lads surrounded him. Bill and Jane were kept busy. Bill certainly was a favourite and Jane thought, no wonder, he must have landed a good catch as he was paying for all of the beer. As the night wore on she looked up at one point to find a stranger watching her pulling the pints. A dark-haired man with a moustache and dressed in the dark navy Guernsey and lilac trousers. Apparently this was a fisherman's dress at that time and Jane did not make mistakes with colours.

It turned out that he swept her off her feet. Soon her name was to be Mrs Forth and they were married at a church on Holderness Road.

Joyce Chatwin

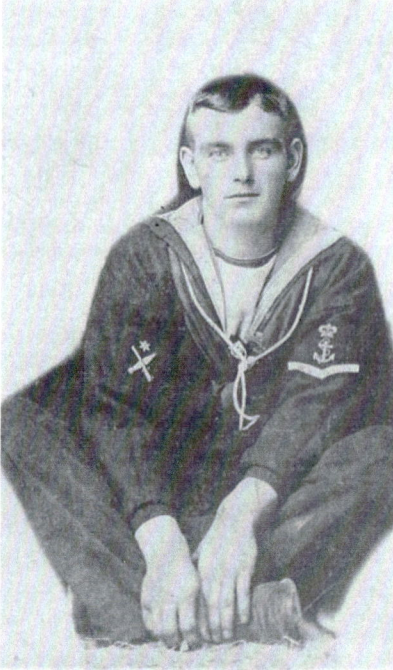

Above left:
William Baker,
lost on early submarines

Above:
William Baker's son
wearing his father's medal.

Left:
Jane's son, Billy Forth

LIFE IS WHAT YOU MAKE IT

After three years of marriage, Jane had given birth to a daughter called Eva and then a baby boy, born with an enlarged heart. The doctors told Jane that it would shorten his life expectancy and that he had not to do anything exerting. This was to be the turning point in Jane's life.

A fisherman's wife only saw her husband once every eight or nine days. So Jane's life was a lonely existence being left to manage on her own and with a sick child. Then she began to notice she was seeing even less of Bill. He told her that he had to stay out longer fishing, to earn more for her and the bains.

She began to see him the worse for drink every trip and the drinking turned even worse as he became abusive towards her and she began to fear for her bains. She found him taking the money that they had to live on. One of the neighbours happened to say to Jane quietly that she didn't look very well and that, "I would be watching that man of yours, if I was you."

The next trip that he made home, Jane was to find her neighbour's suspicions were nearer to the truth than she had first thought or wanted to believe. That same night she heard a noise downstairs, then realising that he was not in the bed she went to the window to see him and a suitcase quietly slipping out of the terrace with a woman. This was to be the blackest night that she had ever had to endure.

In the same terrace opposite her own place lived a chap with two little girls who had recently lost their mother. His name was Walter and his father, Mark, owned a smokehouse.

A week later there was a knock at the door. Jane opened it to find the neighbour from across the terrace, the widower, with his two little girls.

He said how sorry he was to hear the news and handed her a parcel saying, "I hope that you will take this fish."

Jane was only too pleased to have someone to share a conversation with, other than the nosey, next door neighbour. She took the parcel and with that the youngest of the girls began to cry. The chap apologised and said they had better be off, whereupon Jane quickly invited them in, saying that it was warmer inside than out, and offering him a chair and a cup of tea. The two girls discovered Jane's children, Eva and little Billy and soon settled down.

Mark Tether and his dog

LIFE IS WHAT YOU MAKE IT

Things went along a little more smoothly now that they had exchanged names. Jane and Walter began helping each other with housekeeping and meals etc. After a month or two she offered to look after the girls.

One evening Walter came across to Jane's on his way home from work at the fish yard. After picking the girls up he asked Jane if he could see her later when the children were in bed. Jane responded with, "Of course you can," wondering at the same time what on earth he wanted. She was to find out the reason for the meeting when he returned. It was an offer of a job as a live-in housekeeper, if she would be willing to move her and her children across to his house, thus relieving her of rent and any other upkeep of her house.

At first she asked if she could think about it. The fact that she had Billy, her little boy, who had been born with an enlarged heart and a short life expectancy. Jane was quick to recognise the advantages of having a man willing to share her life and so it was that they were soon living across the terrace.

Jane noticed that eyes were raised by the neighbours, with Walter stating, "Sod 'em, all we are thinking about is our kids."

Jane thought to herself that at last things were looking up. Mary and Emily, Walter's two girls, were much older than Jane's Eva and Billy so they became more of a help in the house.

Everything was running smoothly until one evening Walter said to Jane, "I think that it's time that I made an honest woman of you.

Jane put aside her knitting to ask, "What on earth do you mean."

He then replied, "Do you think that I enjoy what you carry about with you every day."

Jane put her head down. She knew immediately that he meant having to live with the name Forth. He went on to say that he had an address for Bill Forth that someone in the fish trade had given him. He told her that he would like to tell Forth that Jane wanted a divorce. Jane was happy but yet hesitant about the idea.

The day came when Walter confronted Jane's estranged husband and father of Jane's children. He pleaded with him and even offered to pay him if he would release Jane from the stigma she bore. Bill Forth had another woman with his child yet he would not lose what he 'owned' and so Jane had to carry that name to her grave. When Walter returned from the meeting he began to swear what he would like to do to this monster of a man. Walter had at least wanted to make an honest woman of Jane and she thought to herself, no wonder she was hesitant about the consequences of the meeting. Jane had learned how life could be so cruel, especially for a woman.

"Never mind Walter," she said, "But do you still want me to stay."

"Of course I do, don't be so bloody daft, we've looked after each other and the bains haven't we? So let's say to hell with him and may he rot in hell."

So that was some assurance to Jane that she still had a home. Life carried on just as before, with Walter working for his father in the fish business, and the only exception being the addition of a baby daughter, called Jennie, and two years later, a son called George. Walter was now in his element. He loved all the kids and would spoil them all rotten, when he got the chance. Young Jennie, aged three and all the girls now wore white pinafores with frills, the fashion of the time. Jane was a dab hand with a sewing machine that Walter had bought her. He found, as time passed, just how competent she was with many things, including cooking, knitting, repairing shoes and even making rag rugs for the hearth. The house shone like a new pin but then something unexpected happened.

Walter came home one night looking very distressed. He told Jane that he had just heard that his cousin, who was married with four children, had died suddenly, with no one to take care of them. Her husband was at sea on one of the many steam trawlers from Hull. Walter sat, head in hands, at the table.

"What are we going to do lass, we can't do anything can we?"

Jane replied, "If you want to bring them here Walt, I'll do what I can until we come up with something when their father gets home from sea."

Walt was very grateful and said that he wouldn't forget this kindness. And so, later that night, Walter returned to the house with the children. They were aged between thirteen years, down to the youngest who was only two years old. Three girls and a boy. They arrived bewildered and very tired, which was only to be expected under the circumstances. Jane had been busy trying to make sleeping arrangements for the extra four children. The numbers in the house had risen from eight to twelve, including Jane and Walter.

It was no easy task that they had taken on. Walt tried to help but found that it was a 'no go' area for a man. This was women's work and Jane was soon exhausted. Thankfully they soon heard the good news that the bains' father was landing the following day. Thank goodness, at last it will all be sorted, Jane thought.

Walter went with the horse and rully to meet the youngsters' Dad at the lock head. He shook hands expressing his sympathy for his loss. The man looked shattered. Then began the questions about his family, who has got them and that he had a funeral to arrange. It all came pouring out and Walt could only look at this man who looked bereft.

"Come on man, give us your kit bag, I'm taking you back to our place and then Jane will tell you what you want to know."

Walter got him inside; things were difficult in such a small space. The youngsters were crying and clinging to their Dad. Jane asked Walt to make a brew and bring it into the front room. She picked up the smallest of his family, then turning to the eldest of his daughters she said, "Take your Dad in the front room lass, then you can have him to yourselves because he'll want to know from you what happened."

At least, Jane thought, we've got this far and we shall soon find out what decision he's come to. Unfortunately this was not the case. He had just gone to pieces, leaving Jane and Walter dealing with everything.

Afterwards when his wife had been laid to rest, he turned to them all saying, "I've signed on again, I'll be off in two days. At least I can earn our keep."

Jane's heart sank as she thought about what arrangements had been made for the youngsters. Walter and Jane were awake most of that evening trying to come to terms with the events of the last few days. They decided to take things day by day, Jane taking her sewing machine out to make the girls pinafores to save their clothes from picking up dirt and so saving time on washing them. The neighbours looked on in sympathy when they saw the amount of washing on the lines strung across the terrace. Walter

Walt Tether
(born 1st November 1876
12.30 am at Hull) who
inherited Mark's business
after befriending Jane Forth

Emily, Mary, Jinnie, George and, Eva, with the orphaned children

began to wish that he had never let Jane offer to take the children but she would not give in, saying, "Leave things be 'til he comes ashore, then we'll sort it out."

Things were about to get worse when news came through that he had disappeared overboard at sea. Walter decided to do something he knew Jane would fight against. What he proposed was to approach the Children's Authorities for information about orphaned children. When Jane found out, she put her head in her hands because she knew just how hard it would be to part with them. As time went by they had to admit that they had done the best they could under the circumstances and the four children were placed in the Seaman's Mission Orphanage.

Walter had to spend more time with his father at the smokehouse. His father Mark, was getting older and it was beginning to effect the time that he could spend at work, therefore Walter was preparing, at some point, sooner than later for him to take the reins from Mark. They began to think about what changes had to be made. Walter's parents had lived in a tiny house fronting the yard. Living on the job with these small businesses was necessary. Very early hours and smoking the fish overnight demanded this.

She was not prepared one day to be told, "You and the bains will be moving to a new house."

"Where?" they all shouted.

"To the yard of course," he said and went on to tell them, "I am having one built in place of the old 'un."

Jane gasped, "How on earth have you managed that?"

Walt tapped his nose and replied, "Leave it to me lass."

The weeks went by and Jane could only wish that the move would come sooner rather than later as she looked at the packing cases ready for the move. She was seeing less of Walter owing to the very early fish landings in a morning. He would return home at night when most of the family were in bed.

When at last they were all installed, Jane first went to inspect her lovely range – her beautiful oven and fireplace in the centre, at one side was the tank with a tap for hot water. The range was the largest that she had ever owned and she began to settle down straight away but the family were all upstairs shouting very excitedly about something. She went upstairs to see what they had discovered.

"Look Mam it's a bathroom!" Something else that she had never had before.

At the front of the house was the shop for fish and with a door that led out of the shop area, which in turn led to the stairs going up in between the living quarters. She couldn't wait to begin putting up her curtains and decorating.

"It's going to be a lot of work girls."

They all nodded and said that they would help. Jane was having to watch her young son Billy, having been told by the doctor that he must not be allowed to do any lifting or get involved in any brawls with youngsters as it could shorten his life still further.

Months later Jane mentioned to Walter that she would like to have her daughter take piano lessons. He consented and the next week a piano sat proudly in the living room, much to everyone's surprise. Eva took to it straight away. So much so that a few years later they were all having singsongs around the piano and young Jennie was playing the mandolin!

Many were the occasions to rejoice but also, unfortunately things were overshadowed when young Billy's heart stopped beating and the household as well as the neighbours went into mourning. Walter himself sat by Billy's bedside sobbing, 'Only fourteen years old, was the lad.'

Jane took it very hard and so the days and weeks followed with much less chatter than usual.

As time wore on, the business was thriving and one day Walter came home and told them that he had bought a new work horse to pull the rully. When Jane went to have a look she was very surprised to find a very handsome beast standing in the yard and exclaimed her surprise,

"Don't you think that it's a bit fancy for pulling a rully Walt?"

"We will just have to wait and see, won't we?" he replied.

The next day was Sunday and Jane had already made plans. In the very early hours of Sunday morning, the household was sleeping; Jane was in the yard with the horse in the shafts of the trap. She led the horse quietly out into the street and keeping hold of the reins she got up into the seat. She got the horse moving away from their yard. So far so good, she thought but by the time they were on Anlaby Road, things became a different kettle of fish, so to speak. The horse decided to change from a trot to a full-blown gallop. Jane had to hold hard on to the reins for dear life. She managed to turn it into Boulevard and by the time they reached Hessle Road she knew - and afterwards admitted - that she had taken on too much. By this time she really had a hard time keeping control. As they sped along Hessle Road, she was gripping the reins as hard as she could and then she decided to turn for home and with a sigh of relief she felt the horse slowing to a trot. She turned the horse into their street, got down from the trap, still holding the reins, then slowly walked it back to the yard. When Walt found out he was not amused.

He shouted at her, "What the hell was you thinking of woman.? You could have been killed."

Her reply was, "I know that now don't I, but I just fancied a run out."

There were many happy events along the way such as the day out that Jane organised as a treat, for all of the children living in the street. Walt was agreeable with the idea as long as he could be excused from the actual event.

It was the summer holidays, which meant that the schools were closed and the kids were running riot in the street.

Jane was getting fed up with the customers complaining about the trouble that the young 'uns were causing and one old lady had had her window broken. Jane was sympathetic about it as she got the odd lad shouting his head off inside the shop door, "Have you got any winkles missus and how's your skate knobs today?" Then the parrot would repeat the same from its cage in the corner of the shop. It had been a hard day and Jane was only too glad when she closed the shop that night.

Emily had given the young ones their tea, with Jane looking over their shoulders, wondering what they had been up to that day but dare not ask.

By the time Walter had finished down the yard and had his tea he turned to Jane saying, "You're quiet, what's up?"

Jane replied, "Well if you must know it's about the young 'uns getting up to no good."

He began to laugh and looking across at her said, "I can't figure you out woman, what the hell can we do about that?"

Joyce Chatwin

Mischievous children in Wassand Street

LIFE IS WHAT YOU MAKE IT

"Well I think we can do something if you'll let me use the horse and the rulley for one day," she said.

"Hold on," he replied, "I will, when you explain to me just what it is that you want it for and that it will not involve me because I will not be included in any part of this venture."

What had put Jane to thinking about even attempting to try, was that earlier that day she heard one of the women in the shop blurting out to her, "It's alright for you, you can afford to take your youngsters on holiday."

Well it did seem to hit a nerve because her plan was to help give the unfortunate young 'uns a good day out, depending of course on the weather. She had to have the yard lads join in and also the women customers that she trusted to keep the arrangement to themselves. And so the plot was set – it had to be a Sunday - the last day of the school holidays. Up to the last few days the destination no one knew, until one of the boys in the street noticed the rully down Walter's yard having a special cleaning job done, thus passing the news around.

So one Sunday, on a summer's day, the folk on Anlaby Road were surprised to hear an accordion playing and lots of children singing. When they turned they were more than surprised to witness a horse and rully with many children and adults aboard and the man with the accordion. This lively, happy crowd on board sang all the way to Beverley Westwood, where they spent the day eating the feast that Jane and the mums had prepared. The horse enjoyed it too, being allowed out of the shafts of the cart to graze on fresh grass, which was something that these working horses very rarely experienced.

Jane had spent many years on her Gran's farm and while she was at the fish yard, she was allowed to use any spare stables to keep goats and chickens.

There were to be many more funny incidents along with the tragedies i.e. when Walter was out with his new rowdy pals, all the worse for wear with alcohol, riding fast through the town in the pony and trap. They were all thrown out of the trap on to some railings. Walter was taken to the hospital with two broken legs and in a very bad way. A vicar was called to read him the last rights but Walter had other ideas and told them to send him away. In terrible pain he muttered stubbornly, "I'll do this

Joyce Chatwin

A day out for staff and families of Walt Tether's Fish Merchants, organised by Jane. The photograph shows Jane, first seated on the front row and Jinnie, third from the left on the second row from the top

myself," and so he did. He did survive this but it took quite some time for him to recover, thus leaving Jane in charge of the yard dealing with the foreman and the bank manager and a sick man for months. It turned out that she became a good manager herself.

Before the accident, Jane had already become aware of changes in Walter's behaviour. He was becoming very irrational, almost as though owning the business had gone to his head somewhat. She was aware of his absence in the evenings, plus the 'new' friends that he had made over the last few months gave cause for concern. He began coming home at night the worse for drink, plus he was suddenly presenting very expensive jewellery to her. Then there was the carpet incident. One day she heard the back door clattering open and Walt shouting, "Mind your backs everybody," and two men rushed through the living room carrying a roll of carpet, with Walt giving instructions for them to take the carpet upstairs and to be quick about it.

Jane asked what was going on and Walt shouted, "Well you wanted a new carpet didn't you? Well there it is!" and he disappeared with the two men.

She began to feel uncomfortable over other matters. One day she overheard him boasting about his winnings. Jane began putting two and two together. She was never a regular church goer but she had always, for instance, kept Sundays as a special day, allowing no work to be done except for preparing meals, and would not have gambling in the house, cards were forbidden. This was how she had been brought up and she kept that day for reading.

The youngsters arrived home from school one day to find, to their surprise, a parrot in their living room. Jane explained to them that one of the yard workers had spotted it on the roof, so Walter sent him up after it. This was a fully grown, very colourful bird and that was not all, it was a talking parrot and a very good one too. In time it learned to say all of their names, plus it knew who the names belonged to. When Jane had to call them from their beds in the morning, the parrot began mocking her. She would shout, "Mary, Emily, Eva, Jinnie and George," and so the parrot would repeat this every morning after Jane. Then she began to realise that as each one appeared, the parrot called one less name! They never did find out where it had come from but it certainly gave them much entertainment.

One evening after tea everyone was there, plus visitors, being the girls' boyfriends. Someone had left the cage door open, and the parrot naturally took advantage and ended up underneath the couch with two of the young men flat on the floor with arms outstretched, trying to capture the bird when suddenly it squawked, "Get up you silly buggers, get up!"

The parrot became a firm favourite of Jinnie and George, plus he entertained the customers in the shop. When the parrot's cage was put in the shop, it then proceeded to mimic all of the street traders, such as the fruit man or the man who sold pots and pans. Then it was the turn of the coalman.

The fun for the kids in the street came one day when, "Coal, a shillin' a bag," was heard and most of the doors opened for bewildered women to find – no coalman, just a parrot!

In the meantime Jinnie and George, still being young children, would relish any kind of surprise that Walt would present them with. A very special one, was the day that he turned up with a very large car, a 7-seater Maxwell, plus a chauffeur to drive it.

"It's for runs to the seaside," Walt told them.

Jane was shocked, naturally, as she knew nothing about it. The chauffeur was a nice enough chap, looking rather sheepish when introduced to Jane, who appeared to him to be gritting her teeth. Later that day when she confronted Walter about this latest 'toy', she was waiting for the usual answer, 'Don't worry, it's all sorted,' but he never explained 'how', to Jane, causing her another headache about finances.

They now had a telephone, which Jane found most helpful. Life continued much like a roller coaster. She never knew what Walt was getting up to.

Once she had got him on his feet again she began to see even less of him. He was presenting her with more gifts of jewellery, saying that they were thank you gifts for looking after him.

The next bombshell came when Walter refused to pay the Council Rates for the house and buildings, the charges for which had risen to new heights. He remained adamant stating that he would go to jail if necessary. That day came when two policemen arrived at the house.

"Trust Walt," the neighbours were saying. There he was, laughing and joking with the policemen until one of the bobbies, suggested that they would have to get a move on and so they went, a policeman on either side of him and Walt was still in high spirits, cracking jokes as if he was going on his holidays.

As they went Jane wept to herself. Emily and Mary, Walt's two daughters disappeared upstairs trying to come to terms with the shame of it all. Eva, Jinnie and George were at school thank goodness but the word soon got around the neighbourhood. Jane tried once again to put things in order, shouting the girls down to help with preparing some food for dinner. At last, she thought, at least I won't be worrying about his whereabouts for a while.

Walt did do a stretch in prison but some said that it wasn't for the non payment of the Rates but perhaps his sentence had more to do with another recent incident when a fish dock 'Bobby' finished up in the mucky water in the dock after a scuffle with some of the fishworkers. It was reported by some of the delighted workers that Walt had been very near the policeman just before he 'fell' in.

Life went on with Jane again holding the reins to the smokehouse, the bank, and the bills - as by the sound of things the country was heading into a war. When they were all around the tea table, the children were naturally asking what they were going to do if war broke out and Jane replied to them to stop their nattering and say to themselves that things can only get better and she made them all repeat it.

One day the foreman over the workers, put his head in the scullery to ask Jane to help with a problem. "The lad washing the herring, will you have a word with him?" Jane went down the yard to find him just lifting a basket of broken herring out of the tub. The foreman nodded at Jane who told him to stand back. She then put on an oilskin apron and showed him how the job had to be done. "Twist the basket in the water then lift it out slowly."

He looked at his basket full of broken fish. He nodded his head while Jane said, "Those of yours will never make kippers, now will they lad?"

Then off went Jane back to her scullery saying to herself, I bet I could do most of those jobs down that yard, then smiling to

Joyce Chatwin

Young Jinnie performing in West Park

herself as she put the kettle on the hob.

Jane began to try to reason with herself about Walter, trying to come to terms with his attitude towards life. He loves the kids but does he feel the same for me? He felt sorry for that poor old soul down the terrace, when bailiffs chucked all her bits and pieces on the road and Walt spotted her sitting outside with her belongings. He soon put that right, he paid the bailiffs what was owing, then stood over them making them put everything back in the house. He always seemed to be full of life itself. But then she pulled herself up abruptly. But what about me? How long can I go on propping him up?

With that she heard the bains coming in from school. She began to feel a longing to be back on Grandma's farm.

The young ones carried on just as before. They were beginning to grow up, Jinnie was seven and George was two years younger. Children lived the same as ever, 'one day at a time', doing their own thing. The schools in the summer would take the older ones to West Park and arrange concerts with a mock stage and any of them with a musical instrument were invited to perform. Jinnie with a mandolin for instance.

At home one day, Jinnie asked her Mum if she and her friends could borrow the rully to make it into a stage. Jane was puzzled when Jinnie told her that it was only the rully that they wanted, not the horse.

Jane said, "That's a relief but the rully is smelly and dirty, it would have to be cleaned."

Two of the yard lads had overheard the conversation and offered to scrub it for the kid's sake, "Go on missus, let the kids have it."

Jane gave in but at the same time, knowing her daughter Jinnie, she was thinking, Wait for the rest of the plan.

It was a Saturday evening in mid-summer. Jinnie and all of the kids in the street poured into the archway next to the house to stand and look upon the rully, now having been scrubbed, furnished and decorated with coloured bunting. Jane had had to join in the preparations of course. The treddle sewing machine had been put into action for dressing up the kids and the rully. The tickets were half a penny for lemonade. Everyone, including the parents joined in, and a good time was had by all...

The Fish Merchants' day out

A 7-seater Maxwell

LIFE IS WHAT YOU MAKE IT

THE ONSET OF WAR

At the start of 1914 war was on everyone's lips. A very difficult and frightening period. Times like these seemed to go over children's heads. The children's games still carried on in the streets, oblivious of tales of war until the zeppelins began to bomb the town, the docks being the main targets.

They closed the fish docks on more than a few occasions, interfering badly with the business. Jane came up with the idea of selling fish on Monument Bridge as she had noticed some stalls popping up there on her last visit. She also noticed the damage around the old town from the last zeppelin raid. Walt agreed to go along with the idea, asking who would be on the stall. Jane told him that if Emily and Mary could look after the shop and the house, they were now sixteen and eighteen years old, then she could tend the stall. She added that he would have to drop her off and then collect her at teatime. He agreed that the stall might be a good idea and that it could be given a try.

All went well for a time until one day they arrived back home to find a queue of women outside the shop, all of who appeared to be hiding something under their aprons. They got inside the shop before this mystery was solved. Emily was reading everyone's teacups! The fee was 2d. Emily would take the cup in her hands and carefully 'swirl it around' to disperse the tea leaves and then proceed to tell the ladies' fortunes.

Jane saw Walter's temper rising and pushed him forward into the living room telling him, "Leave this to me, I will deal with it."

Walt was fair frothing at the mouth at this point shouting, "She must have gypsy blood in her veins!"

With that Jane went back into the shop to find that all of the women had dispersed, not surprising after the sounds they had heard coming from the living room. Emily used to ask her Mam and Dad for their empty cups at teatime and pretend to read the tea leaves. They had all thought that it was a game until this happened in the shop. Apparently her deceased Mum had been known to read the leaves!

Emily, in tears, went up to her bedroom saying she was sorry, with her father shouting after her, "It's the last time that you will be left in charge me lass."

A picture postcard from Eva

Eva as a picture house usherette

LIFE IS WHAT YOU MAKE IT

So that was also the end of Jane being in charge of the stall on Monument Bridge.

Having put this episode behind them Mary, his other daughter, gave Walt and Jane another surprise, announcing that she had joined the Wrens. The women were now joining the war.

Surprise, surprise, when the next day Jane told Walter the news, he cracked his face with a smile and said, "But she can't boil a bloody egg," after being told that she was joining the navy cooks.

As the war progressed, Jane wondered about her future and came to terms with the fact that she owned nothing of her own except Eva and some jewellery that Walt had given her some time back. She had no shelter to call her own, no furniture, no future and she realised that one day she would have to make plans. She told herself the thing that she did have was the knowledge that she had had to deal with the bank managers and lawyers, pulling Walter out of trouble time and time again. His way of living would always be the same. He loved the kids, even to the point where, on one of Jinnie's birthdays, he walked into her classroom, glancing around for his daughter.

He saw her and walked to her desk, and when the teacher asked if she could help him he replied, "It's my Jinnie's birthday and I'm taking her in town to buy her a diamond ring."

The teacher had heard of Walter from Jinnie and told him that this was school time at which he got round that remark by telling her, "But I'll bring her straight back," and so he got his own way once again.

Jane was trying very hard to form some way of life on her own, taking Eva, Jinnie and George with her and how on earth to do it in secret. Surely I think that I would be much happier than I am now, having been let down twice by men. It would be some time yet, she believed.

Walter continued his night life with the boys, visiting many so called, 'Music Halls'. Then he began to bring just one or two friends back to the house, and with Eva now being very good on the piano, they would have a singsong.

When Eva was fourteen, Walt even found work for her taking tickets at the Silent Picture houses. She gradually made pianist for the silent movies.

Things were beginning to get a little better as time progressed but not for Jane, she now knew that Walt was seeing other women. Jane felt she had had enough and began to put her plan into action. She had to move out, especially after what she experienced on one particular night.

It was very late and Jane was in bed when something woke her. The front bedroom was just above the entrance to the yard and she thought that the yardman had forgotten to lock the small door set into the bigger yard gates. As usual Walt was not in the house. She got up and what did she see down in the street but Walter's leg disappearing through that small door. Then the light began to dawn on Jane and she clenched her fists and started downstairs.

This time I've got you Walt Tether, I will not stand any more of your hanky panky, she thought.

With that she quietly opened the shop door and proceeded to lock the small yard door from the outside. She then turned and went inside to wait. Jane had left the front door open and after some time she began to hear whispering, "It won't open, the door won't open!"

Someone was getting desperate Jane thought. Then Walter whispered, "You will have to climb out through the top of the big doors. Go on I'll give you a leg up."

A lady's fancy boot appeared over the top of the door, then fingers, then another leg appeared. Then Jane put her plan into action. She shot outside and grabbed the so-called lady's legs and pulled her down shouting, "Got yer!"

Jane wouldn't let her get to her feet and gave her, as she said, 'A bloody good hiding'. Then she called out to Walt on the other side, "As for you, you won't be sleeping in this house tonight."

Jane thought as she went inside, I will not be shown up anymore. Now was the time to put her plans into action.

The next day, having seen nothing of the gaffer, she took the jewellery that Walt had given her from the drawer, put on her Sunday best and proceeded to the Pawn Shop and turned it into enough money to set her up. Jane had to be assured that she would not get into any trouble for what she was about to do.

The solicitor was the next port of call. When she presented him with the details she then had to think twice about her plan as

LIFE IS WHAT YOU MAKE IT

he told her, "I'm afraid that you cannot remove Jinnie and George, as they are his children, bearing his name."

This was a very big shock to Jane. Now was the time to think with a sound mind. Could she do this? Would they be well looked after? Jane came to the conclusion that there was no doubt that Jinnie and George would be well provided for if they stayed with him because she knew that Walter loved his kids. So she went on to find a little two up, two down terrace house in Strickland Street. She then filled it with second-hand furniture, which she bought from local shops, determined that she would take nothing from Walter's premises but her and Eva's clothes.

She paid the rent for so many weeks ahead and thought that she had done well up to now in executing her plan.

Eva was nearly fifteen at the time and Jane knew that she would have to find work to keep a roof over their heads. Jane had not said anything to Eva as she pondered 'how and when' they could leave. She continued to prepare the terrace house and at that time everyone was making preparations for the 'Peace Parties' as the end of World War 1 had been declared. So Jane of course did her bit, making pies etc. with the menfolk dealing with the bunting.

Jane became more than a little jittery at this point in time for what she had planned as she also knew how it would effect Jinnie and George. She had been removing Eva's and her own clothes in small parcels and taking them to the terrace house.

The day of the street party began early with Walt helping the rest of the men to put tables and benches all down the middle of the road. The kids were all going wild, dressed in bits of red, white and blue. As the evening approached and most of the men had had their share of ale, the music was being played and everyone was enjoying themselves except Jane. It was at this point that she went inside the house for the last time, grabbed her and Eva's things and waited for Eva to approach her from out of the crowd before saying to her, "I have got to do an errand and I want you to come with me."

Eva was approaching fifteen years on her next birthday and looked down her nose but Jane insisted that she would make it up to her and without looking back, they left the street. Jane began to hurry with Eva now asking, "Where are we going and what's the hurry?"

"I'll tell you when we get there," Jane replied, thinking that this was not going to be easy.

After a while she turned into Strickland Street. Eva was now very agitated and asking more questions, as they reached Helen's Terrace and Jane pulled the door key from her pocket and slipped it into the lock.

All of the street parties were still in full swing. In the terrace someone was playing a piano. Jane stepped inside pulling the now reluctant Eva after her and on closing the door said, "This is our home from now on."

Jane pulled some matches from her bag and lit the gaslights, then turning to Eva she said, "If you think this is easy for me Eva then you can rest assured that it has been no picnic."

She then proceeded to tell Eva what had been going on as she now felt that Eva was old enough to understand. Eva naturally asked question after question about Jinnie and George, then turned her attention to the house, asking where was the bathroom etc. with Jane answering, "There are no frills to our little house Eva but I won't be told what to do anymore, will I?"

The next day after a sleepless night, Jane got dressed then looked into the bedroom to find Eva still sleeping. She then went downstairs, bleary eyed and began to make the fire. While doing this, she realised just how sparse the house was with no running hot water and the tap was outside. She had to get used to this all again. Pulling herself together she said out loud, "I've done it once and I will do it again."

Then she wondered if Walter, George and Jinnie had missed them yet. This made her think once again about providing for the two of them. Questioning her own capabilities she thought, Why is it that once again I have chosen the wrong man? We shall never know.

Then with that the fire took hold, breathing warmth into her face and making her feel stronger and more determined than ever. She stood up and went into the tiny scullery to fill the kettle and place it on the fire, saying to herself, At last I feel free.

Back at the yard, mid-morning, Walter was getting dressed after a hectic night. He found that no fire had been made and the place was upside down after the peace party. Emily was sent upstairs to waken Jane and came back down saying, "She's not there and neither is Eva."

After this news Walter went upstairs to question Jinnie and George. Rubbing sleep from their eyes, they both said, "Well, they were at the party."

Jinnie had lain in bed listening to the silence in the house. She had been used to being woken by the raised voices, usually between her Mum, Eva and Emily. She slid out from the warm sheets and went downstairs to find her father Walt sitting at the table with Emily.

Her father beckoned to Jinnie to join them, as Emily suggested, "But maybe they've just gone shopping."

With that Walt shouted out, "And taken all of their clothes with them, I don't think so!"

He looked across at Jinnie asking her, "Do you know where they have gone?"

Suddenly Jinnie began to feel uncomfortable about the absence of her Mother and Eva.

"Please will you tell me who you are talking about?"

"Your mother and Eva," shouted Emily across the table at Jinnie.

Her father joined in, again stating, "They've taken all of their clothes."

Now she began to put two and two together. She dashed back upstairs to check the cupboards, finding them empty and sat down suddenly. She had known for some time that her mother had not been herself. The raised voices, plus arguments seemed to be the order of each day and she also knew that her father could be a very selfish man. She could not bring herself to believe that they had gone off, leaving her without a word. Did she mean nothing to her mother at all? The tears began to flow with anger and she left the house just to get away. The last year had not been a happy one for Jinnie.

'When am I going to get away from it all? Maybe this is the right time, she thought.

This had never happened before and Walt suddenly felt lost. Then he began to feel angry and told Emily to fill the kettle, realising that he would have to light the fire and not being able to remember the last time that he had done it, he shouted, "And bring kindling and coal for the fire," followed by, "Where the hell can they be?".

The next day he knew that Emily would have to take on the housekeeping but in the meantime he was asking the neighbours or anyone connected to the fish trade of Jane and Eva's whereabouts. After the first week Jinnie and George were told that they had gone on holiday but after the second week he had to tell them the truth. That same morning the Headmistress of Villa Place School found Jinnie sobbing outside on the school steps and took sympathy on her, bringing her inside to talk.

Walter was slowly beginning to recognise just how lost he felt. Even the bank manager and yardmen were concerned. Walt had already discovered the missing clothing and jewellery. Then some weeks later someone told him that they thought that they had seen Jane and Eva on Strickland Street. It wasn't long after that, that Jane heard a knock on the door. She opened it to hear a man's voice say, "Thank God I've found you."

Jane thought, Let's get this over and done with, and Walt couldn't get over the threshold quick enough. After many pleadings for her to come back there was no response from Jane and the next thing, he was down on his knees begging and making promises. Jane told him that if she heard any bad reports about him not caring for Jinnie and George she would take them, no matter what the solicitor had said.

After the door had closed behind him Walter Tether, with each step he took, was muttering under his breath, 'What a bloody fool I must be.' But being the foolish man that he was, once he had left Strickland Street he looked up Hessle Road and set off, still limping after his accident, and made for the pub that his mates frequented. Emily, Mary, George and Jinnie would fend for themselves that night.

Meanwhile Jane turned from the door, after locking it. As she turned the coals in the fire, the flames began to dance and Jane lowered herself into the wooden armchair with a sigh of relief. She was suddenly struck with a feeling that she had not experienced for a long time – she was at ease. Her mind began to wander back to the days on Grandma Baker's farm with the animals and sitting up at the table having meals with her Uncles.

Why did I choose two wrong men? she pondered to herself.

LIFE IS WHAT YOU MAKE IT

Then, pouring herself a cup of tea, began to relax by the fireside, dreaming of days gone by and being taken to Hull to see Buffalo Bill's Cowboys and Indians Circus and The Water Circus, all in one show. This travelling Circus docked at Hull. She remembered going to see the parade through the streets of Hull with wagons, real cowboys and Indians, buffalo, cattle and horses, all to perform in a giant ring. Buffalo Bill, whose real name was William F. Cody, was,

"Next to P.T. Barnum, the greatest showman of the nineteenth century... Cody's early life embodies and symbolises the history of the American West. At the age of fifteen he worked as a rider for the Pony Express and in 1864 enlisted in the Seventh Kansas Volunteer Cavalry. He was then employed as a scout for General William Sherman before working under contract for the Kansas Pacific Railroad as a buffalo hunter in 1867 – 68... and acquired the name Buffalo Bill.

When Buffalo Bill Cody came on the first of his three visits to the United Kingdom in April 1887, the furore he created was unprecedented. Thousands lined the streets...

Buffalo Bill would return again in 1891-2 and finally from 1902 to 1904. Places he visited included Hull...

When Buffalo Bill came to Britain... he brought along with a travelling history show with real genuine living exhibits from the western frontier. Cody travelled with a troupe of over 800 people including Annie Oakley the champion lady shooter and many American Indians... The travelling menagerie... consisted of 180 horses, 18 buffalo, elks, mules and Texas Longhorns."

*Extracts from the National Fairground Archive, "Buffalo Bill's Wild West" – The University of Sheffield.

And so it was understandable that Jane remembered such sights for the rest of her life. Another, more gruesome event that Jane would recall was the Airship Disaster of 1921.

The biggest airship in the world, exploded and crumpled over the Humber and could be seen by all for miles around. Forty-four men lost their lives in the tragedy but incredibly five survived.

The following account from the 'Hull Museums Collections' tells the full story of the disaster that would have been the talk of the people of Hull and especially those like Jane who lived close to the Humber.

The largest airship
in the world

R.38 Airship: Disaster Over
the Humber

Airship wreckage

LIFE IS WHAT YOU MAKE IT

THE LARGEST AIRSHIP IN THE WORLD

During the latter stages of the First World War a number of airships had been commissioned by the Government. The order for the R.38 was taken up by Short Brothers at Cardington in February 1919 and work started on what promised to be the largest airship in the world. However, with the end of the First World War, England's economy slumped and the Treasury had to re-evaluate its spending. Naturally this led to problems with the construction of the R.38. (Other airship orders were cancelled and most of the existing airships were either sold off or broken up). Consequently, the order for the R.38 was cancelled and Short Brothers were compensated for the loss of the contract.

Construction Begins

At the end of the war German airships were divided between the European allies as laid out in the Treaty of Versailles. The Americans decided that they wanted a large rigid airship and so the R.38 contract was offered to them in October 1919. For 2.5 million pounds the British agreed to build the R.38 and train its crew and officers.

The Americans agreed and a delivery date of 'late 1920' was arranged. Progress was slow on the construction of the ship and she was finally completed on the 7th June 1921. Because of this delay and the pressure to get her flying there was no chance to change her registration from R.38 to the American ZR2. Therefore, she flew with the US insignia markings on the outer cover and also her British registration R.38 on her first flight, the plan being to convert her to ZR2 when she reached Howden.

Disaster strikes

Doubts about the airships strength arose after she sustained damage during the flight between Cardington and Howden but after her fourth trial flight the R.38/ZR2 was ready to fly to Pulham, Norfolk. On arrival at Pulham the R.38/ZR2 was unable to land as the airfield was obscured by fog and when the fog had not cleared by the next morning it was decided that they should return to Howden and carry out some more trials en route.

Joyce Chatwin

Fish house workers with a ghostly looking Jane Forth, at the back on the far right.

LIFE IS WHAT YOU MAKE IT

It was whilst carrying out this test flight over the Humber on the 24th August that disaster struck. The airship broke into two after the ship seemed to crumple in the middle. There were two explosions in the front section which caused the deaths of forty-four crew. Five members who had been in the tail section survived.

Original reports suggested that the airship had structural weaknesses which caused the crash but the Board of Inquiry offered no technical opinions on the crash. The Americans were offered the R.36 as compensation but it was estimated that they lost almost two million dollars as a result of the disaster. There is a memorial in the Western cemetery on Spring Bank West, Hull, to commemorate all those who lost their lives.

For now Jane knew that she would have to earn a living among the fishing companies. Life went on and Jinnie and George began to visit their Mum and Eva when they were told that they were only a few streets away. Naturally the women workers were very sympathetic for Jane's troubles and so she soon had word that one of the yards was offering her work. Of course, from time to time old customers and fish merchants who couldn't believe what they witnessed discovered her at the bench with the lasses. She simply said, "I have to keep a roof over our heads."

Eva was a young impressionable girl and as time went on Jane discovered that at the young age of sixteen years, Eva was pregnant. A marriage took place between Jack and Eva, and the young husband, who may not have been the father, moved in with them. After the baby was born Jane began to feel somewhat relieved not to have so many commitments. Eva's husband was in work and able to provide for Eva and their child. Many of the women were going off up country to obtain more work. Jane had become a firm friend of two of the lasses that she worked with, when one day the news came that they were signing on themselves to go and, 'follow the herring' and suggested why not Jane? The more that Jane thought about it, the more she liked the idea. I am a free person at last and the baby was now ten months old. The next thing she made sure of was that she would be travelling with her friends. The company in The Isle of Man,

Jane Forth and the Herring Girls in Mallaig, Scotland. Jane is on the left in each photo.

their employers, had them pick up their train and boat tickets and instructions which lorry would pick them up with their boxes at their home address. It was to turn out to be the best free time Jane had ever experienced. The work was hard, sometimes very cold and smelly but she was used to it all by now and did this work for one or two seasons after. Every now and again she sent home a postal order to Eva, to help with the baby. The women followed the herring around the coast of Britain, staying at many fishing towns and villages such as Fleetwood, and Mallaig and Aberdeen in Scotland, and then down the east coast. During this time Eva had given birth to her second child.

Everything continued much as usual for a couple of years. Jane was sat with her two workmates, having their dinner break looking out over the bay at Mallaig when much to her surprise, someone called her over to collect a telegram. Telegrams from home never seemed to contain good news and Jane's heart sank.

With all of the workers looking on she went to the foreman. Fearing the worst she opened the telegram to read, 'Eva in hospital."

When she turned to the foreman he asked, "Is it bad Jane?"

She handed the telegram to him saying, "Sorry, but I must go home."

She made preparations to return to Eva and her family. Jane was to discover that Eva was in hospital due to an overdose. She was also pregnant again and this time to a man in the terrace!

Jane arrived home after a long journey from Scotland by train. She loved being up there, the space and scenery, plus her freedom, but in her mind she knew she would have to return to the housekeeping and her two grandsons. She was made welcome and soon took over the chores. Also the news that Eva would soon be home was a relief in itself.

It was in the days that followed that she began to realise that the numbers had risen in this two-bedroomed terraced house. She had been sleeping in the 'front room' on the couch but she decided to have a word with Eva's husband, Jack. It turned out that it had been turning over in his mind and so it was agreed to look for another rented property. Eva was now back home and she happily went along with their plans, being relieved to have Mam home again. Jane soon heard from friends that there was a

South Boulevard, looking towards Hessle Road, tree-lined and no air
raid shelters

LIFE IS WHAT YOU MAKE IT

larger house to rent, in the next street, Wassand Street.

In no time at all they were installed. The house was on the corner of an archway, down which a glass business operated, under the name of Bennett's. The arrangement was that Mr Bennett's office, at the front of the house, was to be kept clean by the housekeeper. Jane agreed and it wasn't long before Eva was part of the workforce at Bennett's. As time went by, Eva gave birth to another baby boy.

The years rolled by until 1939, the year that war was declared with Hitler and his gang of cutthroats. I cannot and will not believe that this man - if we can call him that - spoke for or represented the whole of the German people. **(EDIT?)**

The war years began to change many things, for instance, a number of businesses were moved from premises that were too close and a danger to the communities who lived in the surrounding streets. We now find Jane with her little brood, having moved house once more, just two streets into South Boulevard, a tree lined avenue, soon to be lined with air raid shelters. On one side of South Boulevard terraces ran the whole length. On the other side large houses with gardens, faced the road. It was in one of these houses that we find Jane and her family. She was over the moon that she had a garden at last and all went well until Eva decided to move in with another man. Jane had no idea that this was about to happen to the family. Eva's husband, Jack, had remained loyal to his family, throughout everything, so now she decided someone had to help Jack keep his family together. Her mind was made up. After speaking to Jack he agreed that Jane would stay with them, after all she had been the one who had raised his children from being small. So a deal was struck.

The years were now beginning to tell on Jane as she watched the air raid shelters being built the whole length of the street, under the trees. Next came the identity cards and ration books. Jane took it all in her stride as usual, being the practical person that she was. She then pulled her sewing machine out, ready to make blackout curtains. She had Jack make her some rabbit hutches and began breeding rabbits for the table. She took over the large garden at the back and started digging for victory. Nothing seemed to be too much trouble for her.

Eva, a beautiful and spirited lady.

LIFE IS WHAT YOU MAKE IT

The air raids began and many nights were spent in the shelters. Young George was on duty during these raids as a messenger boy, going by bike between ARP stations. **(EDIT?)**

Jane had now found her boot last, a heavy metal frame, which had been used to mend the lads' boots in the past and so she was getting ready to do more of the same again.

George began talking of joining the navy when he was 18, which he did in due course. Jane said to him before he left, not to join the submarines. She had already lost her brother, Billy, years ago when they were first experimenting with submarines. He left a widow and two children.

The next one to be called up was Norman, who joined the RAF. Cyril's turn came next and it was to be the navy for him.

Now we come to the time, during the war, when the Government were trying to accommodate a workforce to help repair houses that were damaged during the raids. So they had to find lodgings for these men. They had to find houses with a room to spare and so Jane and Jack had to take in two men who Jane had to give food and lodgings to.

Eva had been living in a terraced house in Boulevard for some time before Jane and her adopted family had become residents. She was now alone with no partner and working in a bakery on Hessle Road.

Across the road at Jane's house, Jane was being introduced to her two boarders. They were given a warm welcome with a good meal, with Jane breathing a sigh of relief. The younger of the two was a young Scot's army officer who had been rescued from Dunkirk and the older man appeared to have a responsible position, engaged with repairing buildings that had been damaged. They were with Jane for quite some time. Of course it did help with the financial situation plus two extra ration books.

A lot of damage was caused in Hull through the air raids, especially in areas backing on to the docks and the railway marshalling yards, which many of the streets backed onto.

During 1942 Jane began to see a bit more of me, her only granddaughter, after I returned from the village of Dunnington near York, that I had been evacuated to. My father wanted to place me in a commercial college in Hull. Thus began a closer relationship than we had had for quite some time.

Joyce Chatwin

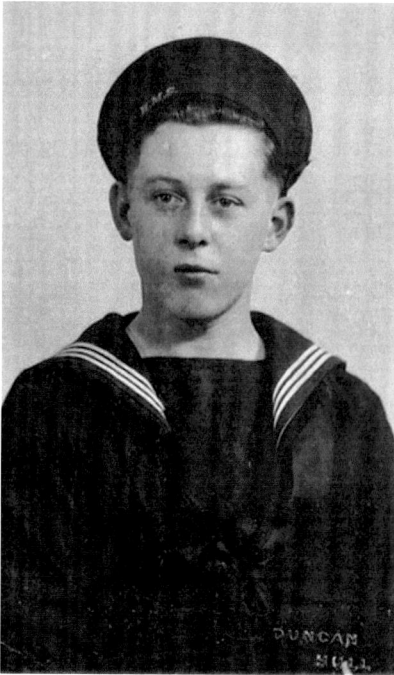

George Hockless,
Submariner

Submariners' Memorial, Gosport

LIFE IS WHAT YOU MAKE IT

Time passed and the lodgers had left and Jane and her son-in-law Jack made the decision to move to a smaller house, due to the fact that her three grandsons were now in the armed forces. So when a smaller house just across the road became vacant, they decided to take it. The day came for the move to the opposite side of Boulevard. After days of taking down the curtains, not forgetting the blackout curtains as they were still in the midst of air raids, she had wrapped all of her pieces of fireside brasses, including the large brass fender that she had lovingly polished over the years. Naturally members of the family came together to give a helping hand and when it came to moving her piano, various friends and neighbours helped. It had been a long day but Jack soon had a fire blazing, the coal having been carried from over the road, seeing as it was rationed!

The house was situated on the corner of a terrace where her sailor grandson George's wife also lived. During the past few years, Janes' family, including her son George and family, daughter Jinnie and family, and daughter Eva, were all now living in Boulevard. It does seem that when families are under stress i.e. in wartime, that they gather to help each other, when needed.

Jane missed her garden, all she had now was a strip of soil running alongside the house, which was now very bare, since the iron railings had to go to the war effort. Jane soon settled in. The piano now had a space in the front room and her fireside brasses shone in their usual place on the hearth. The war continued with the men at home, out each night on fire duty and the usual parade of mums and children carrying blankets out to the air raid shelters.

One day on the front pages of the newspapers came the news, **'The Ship That Broke The Bank of Monte Carlo'**, along with the story that a submarine had actually sailed right into the harbour under the enemy's noses to blow-up most of the harbour buildings and sailed out again. It was even more of a surprise for Jane to discover that it might have been George's submarine, the skipper being a risk taker who was known for his exploits. As the months went by, winter closed in once again with snow and icy conditions and a freezing northerly wind. Coal was still being rationed and people were learning to make their own coal bricks

Joyce Chatwin

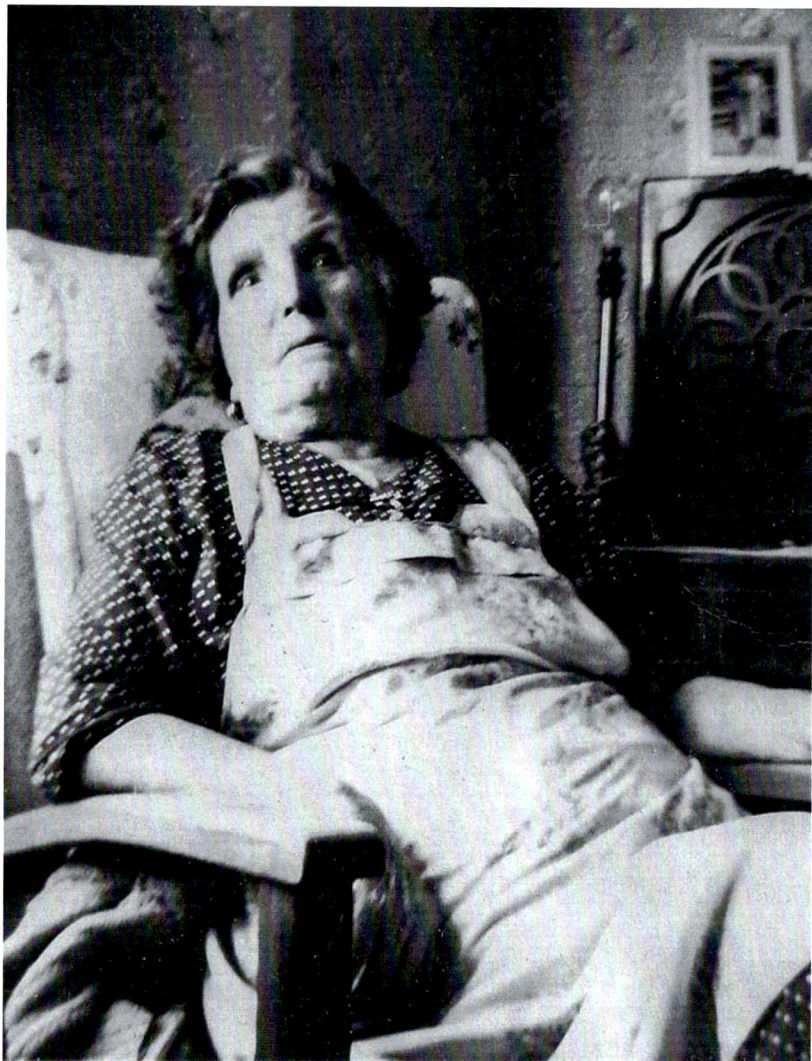

Jane in her chair at 364, South Boulevard

from coal dust. That winter the dock workers were not surprised to see ice floes floating down the River Humber!

Soon the news was that the war was about to turn the corner. The air raids became noticeably less and it did raise people's spirits. Yes, it did appear that things were beginning to turn in our favour at last, until Jane received the terrible news that George's submarine was lost with all hands missing. Eva, George's mother and his wife, broke the news to Jane. In the weeks that followed, one can only imagine the sorrow, with everybody consoling one another. Jack, George's father dealt with it in his own quiet way.

George's two brothers, Norman and Cyril, were serving in the forces when they received the news, Norman was in the Middle East and Cyril at sea with the navy. But unfortunately, later in the war years a telegram was delivered to George's wife that, 'George was missing.' A very unhappy time followed. Jane now had two submariners with their names on the Roll of Honour plaque in Portsmouth, her brother, William Baker and her grandson, George Hockless.

The months wore on until the wonderful day that peace was declared. This news brought about the sounds from all of our ships in port. One could hear church bells mixed with the sirens of the boats in the docks or out in the river, sounds that the people of Hull had missed during the war years.

As the years passed, things like rationing of food, furniture and clothing still remained. It was just inevitable, like the old saying, 'Rome wasn't built in a day'.

Jane had lived through many bad times throughout her lifetime but the worst was yet to come. Her daughter, Eva had been diagnosed with cancer. Jane took Eva back into her house to care for her until her death. She never really got over it. Jinnie had helped to nurse Eva but it left Jane much the worse for wear. So much so that her own health began to fail. Jinnie gave her mother her front room as a bed-sit and looked after her until her death. Grandma had lived with my parents for three or four years, being cared for by my mother.

One day the telephone rang with the message saying that Grandma was failing fast. I remember how quiet the house was as I opened the door to the sick room to be with my Grandma. I went toward the bed to find a very still, silent figure – the

Joyce Chatwin

Jane with her beloved budgie in her daughter, Jinnie's house,
where she ended her days in comfort

opposite of her real self. There was a fire blazing in the grate, just as always, casting shadows on Grandma's belongings; her ornaments, photographs and furniture. I remember thinking that it didn't seem fair that soon she would be taken from us but all her memories covering many, many years would still be left behind. The room was warm and I sat with her for some time before Mam opened the door and beckoned to me. I followed her out, had a cup of tea with her then made the journey home to my own family.

Grandma Jane was laid to rest, with Eva, in the same grave that she herself had organised.

In the weeks that followed, life continued much as before, leaving Mum asking her family if anyone would care to take anything that belonged to Grandma. The most precious item in my eyes was a battered old photograph album. To me, through my Grandma, that treasured album became a bit of 'fairyland' and magic moments, as Grandma disclosed with each photograph different tales, as well as a history lesson.

So it is because of the foresight of a remarkable lady, who realised that very early in the use of photography, it was a way of preserving family history through the eras, of fashions, pastimes, tragedies, and celebrations. So, through an old photograph album's contents, I will attempt to share some memories of yesteryear with my daughter and three sons, plus my grandchildren and great grandchildren.

Joyce Chatwin

Jinnie, born 12th December 1906

PART 2

The Second Generation JINNIE & JAMES HODGSON

This is the story of Jane's daughter, Jinnie. She was born Jennie on 12th December, 1906, but became known as Jinnie. I will use both names for her in my writing. You will recall that Jane had left Jinnie, along with her brother George, with their father Walter Tether.

When Jinnie was fourteen she left school and became a housemaid for the Medical Officer for Hull. She certainly appeared to enjoy her work which was she carried out in a large house in Plane Street, off Anlaby Road. Nothing that she was asked to do seemed to trouble her. In fact she was hyperactive and always had been. She appeared to have similar traits to her father Walt, who apart from his faults was a real joker playing tricks on his mates, etc. Maybe that's how he got away with it all.

When she was sixteen Jinnie was told about a lady with a baby on the way who needed help. When she found out that it was a shop-keepers wife in Wassand Street, she applied and was accepted. She not only kept house, soon she was in her element, behind the counter as the owner realised how efficient and popular Jinnie was, with a great sense of humour. The shop owner was Mr Foster and the Fosters became firm family friends as well as employers. She was encouraged to learn how to pull pints, keeping to the measures etc. and so she continued to serve for many years in between raising her own family, until the street, Wassand Street, was demolished. The owners became her

Joyce Chatwin

friends, as well as the fishermen and their wives and especially the children. To Jinnie it all became one very large family.

On one occasion, I discovered that my mother had baked no less than eighteen Christmas cakes. When asked why, she said it was her bit for Wassand Street! She had offered to make them if the customers brought her the ingredients.

That was my Mum, almost hyperactive. She was to work for this family for forty-two years, on and off, until the shop was pulled down with the rest of the street during the 'modernisation' of Hessle Road. The added bonus to this job was that her mother along with Eva, Jack and the children, lived just across the street where Eva worked at the glass factory. Jinnie, in the meantime, lived with her brother at the fish yard, where Jinnie had become interested in a young man, whom she had 'discovered' from her bathroom window, which overlooked the next door's fish yard. He was a good-looking, auburn haired young man called Jim Hodgson who worked there. As it happened he was also enjoying her attentions and in no time they were a couple.

James Lundy Hodgson, my father, began life on 1st November 1901, in an upstairs room that looked out over the promenade in Scarborough. The house was among a number of fish smoke houses that stretched along a small back road, where the oldest public house in Scarborough still remains to this day.

James was one of seven children born to Elizabeth (Lizzie) Hodgson, nee Chritchison; William, who died aged 18 years in the First World War, James Lundy, my Dad, who died aged 83, Margaret, Ethel, Sarah, Harold and one little girl who died very young. **(NAMES OF PUB AND DAUGHTER?)**

His father was a foreman in the fish houses. This was another very poor family trying to feed and clothe their offspring.

I remember my Grandmother Lizzie taking me, when I was just three years old, to visit her relations who still lived in these premises. She opened a back door into a yard with a small row of lavatories in it, where to the right stone steps rose up to another door to other rooms. We reached this and even as a youngster I was amazed to see a wooden platform reaching over to join another door. It was all very exciting to a small child. Then the door opened and in we went. I remember a lot of women in black and I was given a plate of cold chips! I was too young to understand that this is where my father had lived.

Years later when Dad began to tell us of his childhood, before the family moved to Hull, it was rather upsetting to hear stories about him going to school with his older sister, when he was only two or three years old with cast off clothes and bare feet. This was permitted then to allow the mothers to go out to work.

His Grandfather and Grandmother's surname was Joyce, who kept pigs.

Of course, as the years went by we were to visit Scarborough many, many times and hear Dad's description of times past. On one occasion, as I was the eldest youngster he got me out of bed early one morning, whispering, "Get dressed and we shall go to one of my special places."

I remember the sun was shining and we both climbed up to the castle, looking down on the town and harbour.

Then he said, "Take a deep breath, then you will smell all the bacon frying in the town."

I was to spend a lot of time with my father, especially so when I returned to Hull from Dunnington. Mum was most of the time working in the shop so when Dad presented me with a bike, we used to bike to Pickering Road allotments of an evening, in the good weather, where I must admit I was in my element. I suppose that I became his 'right hand man' while my brothers were still away in Dunnington. I also helped when he decided to keep chickens in our back yard. This meant sheds had to made, so yes, I was sawing wood and measuring up. Fun and games in between college time during the day.

Dad was also enjoying the fresh air, which was a complete contrast to his work place. He was a fish house worker, where fish was smoked, mainly herring, which was split, gutted and washed and dyed, then hung on large nails on long strips of wood called, 'bokes'. These were then carried up into the tall, wide chimneys, which had a distinctive shape from the outside, until all of the open space was filled with hundreds of herrings. Underneath were piles of oak wood shavings and these would be lit and carefully tended overnight, to keep the smoke just right, to produce the lovely golden kippers. I forgot to say that yes, he was a perfectionist.

My other Grandmother on my Dad's side, Grandma Hodgson,

James Lundy Hodgson.
Born 1st November 1901
at Scarborough.

Jim (Dad) Hodgson with Bill,
Jim Jnr and Joyce just before
they were evacuated to
Dunnington

who had been looked after by my parents before leaving us, went to live with her daughter, my Aunt Sarah. Here was another grandmother who had worked with the herring, in between keeping house and raising her family. Everyone called her Lizzie, a small figure who had suffered the loss of one little daughter and many breakdowns. While upstairs delivering her baby, downstairs her daughter fell on the fire and died from her injuries. At the subsequent court hearing, she was excused when the judge heard the evidence.

Life went on nevertheless, with many babies and children suffering illnesses and death due to reasons that today have almost been wiped out. I say thank goodness that we still have the NHS but for how much longer? But the women of Hessle Road had to be as hard as their menfolk to survive.

I became puzzled one day on hearing the name Lundy being mentioned in relation to my Dad, who was called James Lundy Hodgson. The answer is that every first-born son's middle name had to be Lundy. Apparently this tradition went way back through many years, maybe centuries.

As I look back I feel that inspirations I might have had, may have come from my father, who I spent much time with and learned many things of interest from. He was one of those people who would be described as a 'quiet man' who spoke of many subjects, the sky, the earth, politics and the future. Many of his predictions seem to be coming true, for example towards the end of his life he often said that plastics would become a curse to mankind in the future. How right he seems to have been.

Jim and Jinnie continued their courtship in between Jinnie and Jim's houses. Jim lived at 100 Wassand Street with his parents and other family members. He was a good looking young man and away from the fish yard Jinnie hardly recognised him, smartly dressed, shoes brightly polished and he loved dancing.

He was in Jinnie's house one day when the parrot began performing, much to his surprise and amusement.

They were offered rooms by Jim's sister, Ethel, who lived in a terrace close to Jim's parents, in preparation for their forthcoming marriage. The two of them set to work on their future, new home, Jinnie wallpapering and Jim very handy with a paintbrush. Jinnie put up the net curtains and she had it turned

Jinnie and Jim Hodgson

into a little love nest.

Her time spent with Mrs Cash - her first job as housemaid - had been thorough. Spit and polish were the order of the day and antimacassars on chair backs and not a thing out of place.

They were made man and wife on the 27th day of December 1926. When asked by her children, later in life, about wedding photos and a wedding cake, she replied in her usual jovial manner, "Well it was Christmas wasn't it and I think the wedding cake was a currant loaf!"

In those days holidays for the working class were few and far between. So Jinnie and Jim made the most of the Christmas time off, returning to their places of work straight after.

They enjoyed their Sundays, biking to Witherensea with friends. Time went by with Jinnie still behind the counter at Foster's amusing the youngsters and Mrs Foster's baby, who was now 18 months old.

Then one day Jinnie told Jim that she was expecting. They arranged with Jim's mother, Lizzie, who lived nearby, to have the baby at her house as there wasn't enough room or facilities in the lodgings. In the meantime, when Mrs Foster was informed, she decided to offer the happy couple, the house they owned at the opposite corner of the terrace. The front room was a store room for the shop but they rented the rest of the house to them saying, "When that baby arrives you will need more room."

They were more than grateful for the offer and in their spare time in between work, they began to make the home habitable.

I was born on August 9th 1928, delivered by the famous Hessle Road midwife, Nurse Turpin, at teatime, when all the workers were leaving work. Jim's mother helped at the birth and Jinnie told her that she could choose her daughter's name, in return for her help. Lizzie told them that she wished to give her granddaughter her own mother's name, which was Margaret Joyce, Joyce being Lizzie's mother's surname.

When Jinnie was on her feet again, it wasn't long before they moved on to the house owned by Mr Foster, the shop keeper and so Jinnie and Jim went on to have two brothers for me and street life continued to be as lively as before. Jinnie still worked in the shop, part time in between raising her family.

If she heard bad things being said about Hessle Road people,

Joyce Chatwin

A day on the beach at Withernsea.
Kneeling on the far left is Jane Forth. I am on the front row,
second from the right, with my brother Bill two to the left.
My father Jim Hodgson is on the back row, third from the right, with
my mother Jinnie kneeing in front of him.

she would be heard replying, "Yes, rough and ready but with hearts of gold."

Life in the streets certainly was a hard life for almost everyone but things gradually started to improve as a few modern amenities began to appear. One such improvement was where the gas lamps and the streets were lit by the lamplighter who went walking with a long pole surrounded by a small crowd of children waiting for him to push the end of that pole up in the air to poke it inside a glass case at the top of the iron post. They waited, faces upturned to see and hear the plop when the light shone down on them. Although gas first came to the streets in 1822, it was still the principal form of street lighting well into the 20th Century and so the lamplighter was still a form of entertainment for the children in Jinnie's day. Progress was somewhat slower than it is today but the lights down the streets helped people to move around more freely and the children to play out just a little longer.

Another 'modern' form of entertainment was the Crystal Radio, which was commonly known as the Cat's Whisker due to the fine wire that was used to tune it into the few stations that existed. Next was the 'battery radio'. This sound box had a large, heavy battery, which had to be charged at various cycle repair shops, giving Mr Sheard's little cycle shop in Wassand Street some extra trade.

Cinemas, known colloquially as 'Picture Houses' were another form of popular, affordable entertainment at this time. Large buildings were built, enough to seat hundreds of people. At the front was a stage, up through which would rise an organ, with a seated organist playing tunes to entertain the audience before the 'pictures' began.

Between the wars, people also began to be able to afford 'days away at the seaside', travelling by train to places such as Withernsea and Hornsea, which were developing as holiday resorts. Although most people couldn't afford a holiday as we might know it today, cheap train journeys made a day or even a few days away possible. On one such occasion I remember clearly, as a little girl, staying with Mrs Dry in Withernsea, with my Gran Forth, Mam, Dad and younger brother Bill and being joined on one day by a whole host of friends and family. In the

With my cousin George holding my youngest brother Jim (aka Tim)
on the extreme left of the photograph, they appear as part
of a mischievous looking gang of kids.

album is a wonderful photograph that records this happy event in it's entirety.

Life, it seemed, was beginning to turn around for the better, after the General Strike of workers in England for better wages and conditions. It didn't appear to make things much better for workers living in the streets of Hessle Road though. Youngsters still played out in bare feet but they never complained, only when they were hungry. Children always lived in a child's world, not that of their parents, which they didn't really understand. They knew that you got a sweet at the sweet shop and sometimes 1d for going an errand and if you waited until closing time at Stipetic's Ice Cream makers, down the street, you could get a mug of ice-cream for 1d. Sometimes the lady who sold hot cakes from her house would give them one but the time that the children got really excited was when the fishing trawlers landed because most of these youngsters were born into fishing families. It was usual for their fathers, brothers and uncles to bring home in their kit bags some sweets, toffees and such like from the trawlers bond.

Sadly, there were also times when some of these men did not return. The neighbours never failed to come and aid the bereaved families. Toys were few and far between and the kids learned to amuse themselves, making games with marbles and sticks and stones or whatever else came to hand. They would even make a ball out of rolled up newspaper.

Jinnie continued working at the shop, nightimes and weekends when Jim looked after the youngsters. She had a fondness for these Wassand Street young 'uns. But she couldn't help making mischief with them and one Saturday a small group of lads burst into the shop shouting, "Have you any boxes Jinnie?"

Jinnie said, "No , but I know who has."

With that the lads began jumping for joy. The customers in the shop watched Jinnie as she told them, "At the top of the street you will see a big yard opposite Mr Sheard's shop, go in there and they have some with handles."

As they disappeared a customer was heard to say, "You rotten sod, she's sent them to the undertakers!" and a burst of laughter issued from the shop.

Things may have looked brighter but the depression that was waiting took away their hopes. Many workers lost their jobs, thus less money meant that the gas meters were ignored and people put the kettle on the fire once again. When the summer weather returned, the women did their knitting, and braiding fishnets for the trawlers, outside their houses in the sunshine. The children would help by filling the bobbins for their mothers. As time went by Jim made use of the attic by breeding canaries, beautiful yellow songsters that people would hang outside in fine weather in their cages. So the birds kept singing but things were about to change for Jinnie and her family.

Jim's parents, especially his mother was having a hard time. Jim's brother, Harold, broke the news to Jinnie who straightaway went to see Lizzie. She opened the door to witness her mother-in-law in a very distressed state and told Harold to bring the doctor.

The doctor arrived only to tell them that Lizzie would need someone to give her constant attention because she had suffered a mental breakdown. Jim had arrived just before the doctor and looking at Jinnie for help, she nodded her head knowing only too well that this was not going to be easy. I was now eight years old, Billy was four years old and Jim, known as Tim to family and close friends, was one year old. There was nothing else for it, they would have to move in with her in-laws and leave their own house. **(EDIT?)**

After the first few weeks they both began to realise just how much work and worry lay ahead of them. Two sick parents and now Jim's mother Lizzie was mentally ill in hospital. Thank God I've got Jinnie he thought, she seems to take it all in her stride.

In no time at all she had organised the sleeping arrangements, which were that his parents moved into the downstairs front room, Jim's brother, Harold, into the back bedroom, he and Jinnie and the baby, Tim, aka Jim, into the front bedroom and Billy and I into the attic. I was the eldest and saw it all as a big adventure. I had only experienced helping to feed my Dad's canaries up in the roof and so looked in amazement when our beds appeared up there and immediately went to tell my brother Billy.

So far, so good, until Lizzie began begging to be taken home.

Jinnie could not refuse and during the days that followed, weather allowing, Lizzie had the odd outing with little Tim sitting on her lap in the wheelchair.

Gradually things were improving. Jim now had his 'cat's whisker' radio to play with, Billy and I had our cousins to play with down the terrace, which was at the opposite end of the street, opening out onto Bank End. Really called Goulton Street, it got it's other name because it opened out onto a road which lay on the edge of the railway marshalling yards and across to the banks of the Humber. I found to my delight that if I climbed on a chair in the attic and opened a window in the roof, I could see the marvellous vista that lay down below, stretching across the railway tracks and the docks to the Humber and across further to Lincolnshire.

I was now allowed to go to see the matinee at Langham picture place on Hessle Road on a Saturday.

Our address for a while had been 100 Wassand Street but things were about to change once again when Jim asked Jinnie one evening, "What do you think about us moving?"

After a long pause, she put down her knitting needles and looking at Jim answered, "I don't understand just what you mean Jim by 'move'."

His answer was, "To move out of the streets for all our sakes, to where there is a bit of fresh air."

She answered that she needed time to think about it. When she had, she could come to no other conclusion but to agree because he could talk about nothing else but this house with a garden for rent. And so after a few weeks we find the family, plus Lizzie and Bill, Jim's parents, moving into Anlaby Park Road South with a garden and a bathroom. The house was situated next door to a small shop owned by Mr Bailey and his wife. The houses looked across at large fields and nearby was a small road called Lynton Avenue, with a large fishing lake at the end.

At the back it continued on to the allotments with one to let. Of course we might know who was a very tired Jinnie but she took it all in her stride. Jim soon had the allotment in hand as he was determined to help feed the gang.

I had to go further to my school which was in Pickering Road. As time went on things began to change. For instance the old folks felt that they were lost being away from Hessle Road and their neighbours. Jim's father had become worse with his illness, plus they had all had to tighten their belts because they were paying much more rent. Jinnie couldn't work part-time at Foster's shop and the only transport they had were two bikes. I went to school on one and Dad had to go to work on Hessle Road on his, which meant it was bus fares for Jinnie to get groceries.

Builders had started to build new houses nearby and were asking for women to scrub them clean to sell. Jinnie decided to go, leaving Timmy, now two years old with Lizzie. She found that the work was exhausting as she was still running the house and cooking in the evening with hands that were red raw. She became ill and Jim decided that enough was enough and so they returned to live on Hessle Road.

The evening before the day that we moved, my dad asked me if I was sorry to be going back and was surprised when I replied, I wasn't sorry because they had a swimming baths and Langham picture place to go to on a Saturday morning. He couldn't deny me that.

Our next house was in Wellstead Street, first across from Wassand Street. At the end of Wellstead Street, I now discovered the back entrance to my old school, Constable Street and I soon realised that I only had a few yards to walk there.

Jinnie soon began to pick up, as her friends plus the kids in Wassand Street welcomed her back. The house was much larger than she had expected but as usual she had to roll up her sleeves and soon the beds and curtains were up.

After the youngsters and the old folk were in their beds, her and Jim sat with a cup of tea, with Jinnie sighing, "Home again at last and you won't have as far to go to work anymore."

Everything went well until the death of Jim's father. With his passing away, Jim's mother took a turn for the worst, with her mental disorder. Jinnie was with her at night and she could hear Lizzie crying out for the little girl that she had lost in a fire, many years ago. She could not be pacified until Jinnie decided to take me to her. I was sleeping upstairs, so a very sleepy little girl was taken to her Grandma, who was still upset until Jinnie whispered to me, 'Climb into bed and lay with Lizzie."

This I did and with that I was drawn into Grandma's arms

with the words, 'Come to me, I'll keep you warm.'

Soon all was quiet again. Jinnie heaved a sigh of relief and on leaving the room, turned out the light after looking at the two sleeping figures in the bed, the old one cradling her granddaughter in her arms.

When Lizzie recovered Jinnie was surprised, one day, to hear me asking, "Is it alright if I go to Scarborough with Grandma?" and things began to settle down once again until the newspapers made their readers sit up.

During the next two years it became evident that a German called Hitler was a troublemaker, who was bent on causing serious trouble. During this time plans were being made by the Government to help to protect the children for the future years against what was now expected – war!

In the early part of 1939, the general public were informed about plans being put forward regarding various regulations i.e. black-out curtains, blacking out roads and streets, rationing of food, clothes and furniture and much more, air raid shelters, identity cards and teenagers with bikes to act as messenger boys riding between ARP depots. This was soon followed by trials of the air raid sirens in the towns.

Parents, including Jinnie and Jim, now had to decide if they wished their children to be evacuated out of danger. Jim could see how it was affecting Jinnie, who was crying herself to sleep like many other mothers. The decision was made to let the two elder ones, Bill and I, who had just had our birthdays aged 11yrs and 8yrs, go. They signed the forms on condition that their two children were to stay together.

All went well until Jinnie received postcards, mine was from Scarborough and Bill's from Dunnington near York. After this shock Jinnie was so distressed, Jim decided to borrow the firm's carrier bike to go and see for himself, and so one Sunday he rode the sixty-plus miles to Scarborough and the following Sunday he rode a similar distance to Dunnington to put Jinnie's mind at rest.

In the weeks that followed, after I found Billy's address through letters to and from my mother, I decided to ask my mam, "Why can't I go to my brother?"

Thus the wheels were set in motion and it was agreed that I would join Billy in Dunnington. The day arrived for Jinnie to collect me from Scarborough on the Saturday. The large house had the name 'CHILDHAVEN' and before the war had been a charity for poor mums to take their children on holiday. So began another chapter finding Bill and I together at the same address. Jinnie went back home to Jim, a much more contented lady.

Within the next few months Jinnie heard of a house in Boulevard, next door to her brother George and they decided to take it, seeing as her mother Jane, lived close by. Jim's mother Lizzie decided to move in with Sarah, one of her daughters. The war seemed to be causing families a need to be closer together. But news of the war was not good. The next thing to happen was to line the whole length of Boulevard, down each side, under the trees, with large brick air raid shelters filled with wooden bunks. A couple of years or so later, these shelters were often found to be full of women and children. The older men had to do 'Fire Duty". Jim was one of these men and one night Jinnie and Tim, now aged five, had a bad experience during one of the worst bombing experiences of the war.

The bombs were dropping all around when suddenly a huge blast nearby came into the shelter. Jinnie threw herself across the baby to protect him but she received the blast and lost her voice for some time – thus asking for Tim to be placed with his brother and sister. Jinnie had to get her third child away from the danger that they had just experienced. Fortunately, the couple that had taken Bill and I, having no children of their own, were only too pleased to have young Tim. Arrangements were made after Jinnie had a word with a lorry driver that she knew, who did the York run, to transport Tim to Dunnington, as it was imperative to have him placed in safe hands. His foster mother was there to welcome him and so were his brother and sister after school. Jinnie was informed of his arrival and she gave a sigh of relief. She was then, once again, behind the shop counter, to help pay for the three children's care away from home.

We began our new school at Dunnington near York and soon settled down. It was a Church of England school and was just across the lane from their house.

I got into letter writing to my parents and was soon writing everything about our house. I went on to say there was a bathroom, and hot water if someone pumped it from a small hand pump in the kitchen, from a well just outside the front door. Our foster home had two white Sealyham Terriers called Mick and Chum. As my mam began to get these letters it helped put her mind at rest.

When Doll, our foster mother, hadn't enough sugar to make jam for us, Mum would appear, just for the day, armed with anything that would help to feed or clothe them. One of the perks of working in Foster's shop was that she had access to the growing 'black market' and could often get plenty of rationed goods for her family.

Being in the country, everything such as fruit and greens was fresh and plentiful. That winter found us with two white enamel buckets in our pantry, full of plum jam.

As the letters continued, I enjoyed sharing village news, such as that about a farm called Buckles Farm, which was in York Street, where you could catch the bus for York.

It was our favourite place because a lady called Aunt Lill, along with her sons and daughters lived there and taught us many things, such as feeding the calves and chickens and helping in the dairy where we learned to separate the cream from the milk to make butter. They had two horses and three milking cows, plus calves and bullocks. One such letter arrived telling our Mam and Dad that one of the horses had had a little foal, which she called Prince. I let them know that they now had a pigsty in the garden and chickens and a boiler to boil potatoes, known locally as tatties, for the pigs.

I kept them informed about haymaking and threshing time, with a large machine taking the corn from the sheaves. This was when the farmers got together with horses and carts to help one another. In the autumn, when it came to harvesting potatoes, children who were old enough were allowed time off school, so I volunteered. I wrote home to say that Toddy (Doll's husband and our foster father) had got me a bike, with which I could get to the fields, which were sometimes miles away. I wrote; 'Toddy is now a Gang master finding workers and working alongside them.'

One bad winter when we couldn't go home for Christmas on account of the air raids on Hull, Bill, Jim and I learned all about what the village and the school did at Christmas. I wrote home that, 'We are all making decorations for Christmas in the Reading Room, where we have a party with Lord and Lady Hunt, who live in an enormous house with lots and lots of gardens on York Road'.

The next letter was to tell them that I was going to be in the Christmas play where I had to dive under a table! All the girls had to make costumes to be judged at the party. I said that I was making myself a W.A.C.'s (Women's Air Corps) hat.

The day of the play and the party arrived along with Lord and Lady Hunt and a friend of theirs from New Zealand, in an army uniform, a Lieutenant no less, Lt Warsnop. He was on leave and staying with Lady Hunt and her brother.

A few weeks later, I wrote home saying that they were having a competition at school about New Zealand because the soldier at the party had left some books as prizes. I also told them about the weather and that Toddy had to dig us out of the snow to get us to school. It had reached to the top of the back door! After weeks of snow and more snow, I wrote home that, 'At last we can see out of the windows again,' and 'It's a good thing that we have fires in the classrooms to help to melt our bottles of milk!'

I was soon in my element again as the spring sunshine arrived and I wrote that we would be able to come home for Easter and then went on to tell them that I was helping Toddy to feed the pigs and the new calves at the farm and also that Doll had told me that I could have a bit of the garden that I had asked for.

Then came the next bit of news as I wrote to tell them of my success in wining one of the book prizes from the soldier from New Zealand. The prize book was called, 'England and The Maori Wars.' Lt Warsnop wrote to congratulate all of the prize winners from his camp in the Middle East, which was so exciting for a young girl, living away from home herself.

Unfortunately I lost the book and the letter, during a house move but with the help of my offspring I have recently managed to track down the home of Lt Warsnop in New Zealand, to a place called Katikati and to get hold of a 1st edition of the book to replace the lost prize.

We were allowed home for short stays during the school holidays and were so surprised, after being met at the bus station, to be told, "We don't live in Wellstead Street anymore." Then seeing the frowns on our faces, mam went on to tell us where we now lived, which was Boulevard, and as youngsters do, we took it all in our stride.

The war years carried on but like most towns on the east coast, especially those with dockyards, the people somehow coped. Whenever any of the men in the forces came home on leave, you could bet your bottom dollar that there would be parties held for them, especially on Hessle Road.

Jinnie and Jim, like everyone else, went from day to day, Jinnie behind Foster's counter, swapping tales with the tradesmen while trying to console mums and wives who had received 'bad news' in a telegram.

The trawlermen were still going out to feed the hungry and many lost their lives doing so. They still had the cinemas to go to and the fish and chip shops, which were not rationed, and their wirelesses. If, while in the cinema, an air raid siren was sounded, it came up on the screen to warn the audience but there were never that many who left their seats and this life continued until peace was declared in 1945. **(CHECK-YOUNG JINNIE?)**

It was around this time that young Jinnie was allowed to visit with her own school friends and go into the town centre. She was about to witness a scene that she never forgot.

Looking down Princes Dock from Monument Bridge in the centre of town, she saw a ship discharging its cargo. She stopped in her tracks and turning to her friend asked her to come and see what was happening on the dockside. Her friend told her that they were looking at refugees escaping the war in Europe. Jinnie was appalled to see that they were wearing sacking on their feet instead of boots and they looked very, very ill. Later when she reported what she had witnessed to her Mam and Dad, she was told that a lot of these people were Jewish, like our neighbour next door and trying to explain about different religions that people followed but that many of our neighbours and shopkeepers were welcomed into our streets. Hessle Road had many shops and businesses that belonged to people of the Jewish faith and we found that they welcomed us into their shops because they were a friendly lot, just the same as ourselves.

My Dad had a Jewish friend who was a barber and he once remarked to me, "If you were to walk in a Jew's footsteps you would not go far wrong."

My father was not a religious man and I never forgot his words. I also remember my mother telling me that it was a Jewish lady who offered Jinnie her own veil on her wedding day. Mum gladly accepted it and told me that it was pink.

To this day, there is a reminder of the transportation of refugees from Europe, in Hull's Paragon Railway Station. There is no visible Platform 1. It does exist but is outside of the station. This platform is not used now but it and the immigrant waiting room can still be seen,

"For those leaving the main Paragon Railway Station, the separate railway platform and its emigrant waiting room can be seen to the extreme left of the railway station as one travels out of Hull on the transpennine railway service that once conveyed emigrants on their way to transatlantic ocean liners. A living memory to the millions who spent time there on their way to a better life."

Hull was only a 'way through' for many refugees as they travelled to Liverpool and then on by boat to America and Canada.

THE POST WAR YEARS

The family, now being re-united, there were parties as one might imagine but rationing still had to continue.

In 1944, Jinnie and Jim decided to exchange houses with someone they knew, for a larger one in the Boulevard. It was a front house situated at the end, looking all the way down Goulton Street, (known to us all as Bank End). Jinnie still continued serving and amusing the customers. Plus she had her three children back together again, making a lot more work for her.

Over the next few years they began going to Scarborough whenever they could, eventually daring to go further afield for weekend outings. Then Jim surprised Jinnie one day when he announced that he had bought a car. The next day, an Austin 7 with a maroon body and black mudguards was standing on the road outside.

Jinnie just stood there, repeating the words, "I don't believe it, I just can't believe it," and Jim said, "Well don't just stand there, come outside and see it properly."

LIFE IS WHAT YOU MAKE IT

When she arrived back at the shop it wasn't long before the customers were commenting that, "Jim Hodgson has bought a car, can you believe it?"

Of course they were ready for the usual comments such as, "Good luck to them," - "Lucky sods," - "They deserve it," and so on. Jinnie worked even harder to put her pennies away for the petrol. Jim already had his license from years gone by for a motorbike and sidecar, which he took Jinnie, then his girlfriend to Withernsea on.

The months that followed found them visiting different areas of England. One such trip was to a cottage at the top of a steep hill, set in a line of what had been iron miners' cottages from way back. The name of the village was Rosedale, still a lovely place to visit today. After one trip away, when arriving home a day earlier than expected, Jinnie and Jim explained that they had found it a lonely place with only one neighbour to talk with. She was the cleaning lady at the village public house, way down the hill. When asked how she managed during the winter months, Jinnie was told that the neighbour tied sacking round her legs to climb back up the hill! Apparently during their stay, the sheep would gather round the cottages and so on their last day Jinnie gave them a treat by throwing them slices of left over, cut bread, slice by slice, much of which stuck to the sheep's woolly coats and she said with a smile, "They looked just like little Christmas trees running down the hill."

Rationing had come to an end and shops were starting to stock up once again. Slowly more cars began to appear on the road and hence more families were making for the seaside, including their grandchildren.

The summer holidays came and the prospect of going to live in a caravan for a whole week, by the sea, was just the most exciting thing for the children, which they never stopped talking about. They didn't mind having to go to bed anymore because they could dream about it and they dreaded Mum shouting up, "If you don't quieten down you won't be going," and that would be the end of any disturbance.

Jim had now given up his allotment and his chickens from the pen in the back yard, all of which had kept the family in fresh

My Dad Jim with his first car, taken from the bedroom window of their house on the corner of South Boulevard and Goulton Street.

foods during the war.

The car came in handy for giving Grandma Forth a day out with Jim and Jinnie.

Wallpaper was back in the shops and Jim was soon to find out when he returned from work one tea time, to find Jinnie standing in the middle of her newly wallpapered living room saying, "I'm just finishing painting the doors, tea won't be long."

He couldn't help chuckling to himself because there she was in her element – paint pot in one hand, paint brush in the other and paint on her face, all down her hands and arms, pinafore and shoes.

Jim turned away calling, "You've done a very good job Jinnie." She was known to do many jobs in half the time of anyone else.

Life went on with Jim still working as a fish smoker, which had now become a night-time job as there was much more fish being landed. There was talk of building more trawlers as men had returned from the war and conscription.

Councils were now building more council houses and ruins left from the air raids were being cleared. Hessle Road was returning to its hustle and bustle once more, with cheerful shouts of, "Are you spending another club cheque at Clothing House Sissy, I'll be telling on you", and then would come laughter from the crowd. These folk had a sense of humour bar none. They would take it as well as give it, even when things weren't going too well.

Things were beginning to change for Jinnie and Jim and eventually their daughter's little family moved to Hessle, after a year of saving for a deposit to own their own house. Yes it was hard but it had been decided by the Government, in order to help young couples achieve this, that whenever the purchase of a house was made, the taxes taken from a man's wages, would be cut for two years to help them make a start. So Ken and I bought our own house and moved to where there were better schools for our offspring.

As time moved on, there came the news that houses were being built to house the residents of Hessle Road, as the streets and terraces on the fish dock side of it were to be pulled down. This included, South Boulevard, Wassand Street, Eton Street,

West Dock Avenue and many more historic sites. Many of the inhabitants, who wished to stay down Hessle Road, were quickly arranging with their friends, who lived on the opposite side of Hessle Road which was not to be pulled down, to let them have the new houses. It so happened that Jinnie's landlord did not wish to let them exchange. He said that they had been perfect tenants for any landlord. Then their son Bill, and Betty, his wife, were now in a position to help. Jinnie and Jim, who was now retired, were taken to a modern house off First Lane, Hessle to find out if they approved, without knowing anything of Bill's plans.

Jinnie and Jim later said, "You could have knocked us down with a feather," after the deal was done and they had a new house to move to.

So the removal date came around, everyone helping them to settle in, Jim giving his new garden and garage the once over, saying to Jinnie, "It's just the job."

Their daughter and family having been settled in Hessle for some years, were just walking distance away, plus they were on the telephone in case of illness or other emergencies.

Things were going well until the Government decided to start making cutbacks, closing mines, docks etc. and the fishing industry was beginning to collapse due to the third of the 'Cod Wars' with Iceland, and many began losing their jobs and businesses. This effected hundreds of families, including their daughter's family, three of whom were made redundant.**EDIT?**

Ken had already lost his 'fish round' that he had been running since leaving his job as a bobber and filleter on St Andrews Dock some years earlier and had been made redundant from a series of factory jobs that he had obtained.

Everyone became despondent and so plans had to be made and it came as a surprise one day, when Ken decided to get out of the rat race, and suggested to his family, "How about we move to Scotland?"

They had spent many holidays in Scotland, camping and caravanning but of course it still came as a surprise to Jinnie and Jim, plus it didn't make it at all easy as I had to break the news to them. They just had to accept what was about to happen to part of their family. I promised to write regularly, which she did.

LIFE IS WHAT YOU MAKE IT

Ken and I, and our youngest son, went up to Scotland to look for possible houses to buy and finished up choosing a croft on the Isle of Skye. The move took place in October with a promise that we would make a visit, back down from Scotland at Christmas.

Jinnie's two sons and wives and respective families, continued to look after them both, which gave me peace of mind. During the year of 1982 I was to make many journeys back to Yorkshire and my mother began to worry about it. Then, come October, she welcomed some of her daughter's family back home, once again. **(EDIT-TIME?)**

Many were the days that all of the families spent together on holidays, with Jim teasing everyone and singing old music hall songs, while Nanny, as all the kids called her, playing tricks and having sing-songs, which they all loved. In fact Nanny's house soon became a favourite place to spend weekends, when cousins would all get together. As they became older this closeness for their grandchildren was such that it never left them and in fact they were more than pleased as it brightened their days.

As time went by we approach the grandchildren's teenage years but their love for 'Nanny and Granddad' never diminished.

In 1979, their son Bill and daughter in law Betty moved to buy a shop in Withernsea and after a while they decided to offer Jinnie and Jim the choice of them living in Withernsea and they moved to a lovely bungalow. Jinnie and Jim were delighted with their new home, especially when they saw the garden and greenhouse. So it wasn't long before they were installed and it also wasn't long before the grandchildren, plus two great grandchildren were all appearing at intervals.

Jinnie and Jim loved their time in Withernsea, with the fresh sea air but a sad event was to cloud their lives when one day Jim collapsed at the bus stop in Withernsea. When the doctors investigated it was not good news. Jim was diagnosed with cancer of the lung. One of the doctors asked Jinnie about Jim's working years and was not surprised to hear that he had worked in the smoke houses, curing kippers. Unfortunately there was very little that could be done and Jim passed away, on 16th November 1984, at home with son Bill and wife Jinnie at his bedside, aged 83 years.

Joyce Chatwin

Jinnie Hodgson, nee Tether
Born 12th December 1906
at 138, Adelaide Street, Hull

LIFE IS WHAT YOU MAKE IT

Jinnie took it very badly. So much so that Bill and Betty started bringing her to their shop and it did the trick. She was back behind the counter of a shop where she could enjoy the chat with the customers. Life carried on like this for Jinnie for a couple of years, until Bill and Betty decided that they had to give up the shop and Post Office, due mainly to the fall of customer numbers.

As it was with a number of other East Coast holiday towns which began to decline after the closure of the Hull and Holderness Railway, which began with the 'Beeching's Axe' in the early 1960s which chopped off a great number of branch lines from the main trunk routes, including the one that ran through Withernsea.

One day, Betty suggested to Jinnie, the idea of them moving in with her to take care of her and this was to be as the years were now catching up with her. Next the shop was sold and the three of them moved back to Hull together to a house just off Anlaby High Road, where despite her deteriorating health, Jinnie lived out her years with the comfort and support of her family.

The move meant that they could move back to their old family Doctor's practice at the Hessle Road end of North Boulevard.

The move also made it possible for me to see my mother more often and to spend valuable time with her, as did her extended family with grandchildren and great grandchildren visiting regularly.

Words cannot express the gratitude for the care that Betty gave Jinnie in her final years.

Mam died in 1987 at the age of 86.

(EDIT-NOT IF SHE WAS BORN IN 1906)

Jinnie and Jim Hodgson promenading along Scarborough Front,
one of their favourite places in later life and Jim's birthplace

PART 3

The Third Generation JOYCE & KEN CHATWIN

It was now 9th August 1928 and I popped out, safe in the arms of Nurse Turpin, with Grandma Lizzie Hodgson looking on. Jinnie, my mother asking, "What is it?", and the answer came from Grandma Hodgson, "It's a girl lass". Jinnie now relaxed and smiling lay back on the pillow, with her daughter in her arms murmuring, "Wait until your Dad sees you my girl."

She was the first of three children born to Jinnie and Jim Hodgson who lived on the streets backing onto the railway marshalling yards running alongside the docks, 17 miles in all.

The fish docks *(St Andrews)* were roughly 1.5 miles long with the largest fishing fleet in the world in 1928.

This was a working class area known in certain educational centres as "the village within a city". Three of the streets, Strickland Street, Wassand Street and Walcott Street were nicknamed, 'Faith, Hope and Charity and it was in one of these three that I was born.

The streets were only a very small part of Hessle Road. This was the workplace of thousands of fish workers and their families. With most of the men being away aboard the trawlers most of their working lives leaving their wives to raise their families and look after the elderly.

These crewmen were at sea fishing for three weeks with only two days at home in which to land catch and draw their wages sometimes landing in debt to the trawler owners when it was a bad catch or too many trawlers landing their catches .

A dangerous job, especially when the wages were a gamble and thousands of these men were drowned at sea over the years.

This is part of the background that I was born into like hundreds more in the streets around Hessle Road, all fighting for their livelihood.

Father - James Lundy Hodgson

Mother - Jenny (Jinnie)

Children - Margaret Joyce, William Lundy and James Walter

Not only the men worked with the fish, many of the women belonging to these families worked with the herring, some of them travelling round the coast, even over to the Isle of Man and up to Scotland. They sent money back to their families who were being cared for by relatives. The work was sometimes bitterly cold working in cold water out in the open on the dockside in all weathers. Before they set off from their lodgings they had to bind their fingers with strips of rag so they could avoid cuts from the razor sharp gutting knives.

Both of my grandmothers and some of my aunties also earned money this way. My Dad worked mainly in the smoke houses where they smoked the herring in giant chimneys over fires of oak chippings. The end product was the famous kipper.

As the years passed, I was to discover that there was much more to my father than a fish smoker. We were both very close.

As we have already heard, my Mum Jinnie had had very mixed experiences as a child. Born out of wedlock, so to speak, her father being in business as a fish smoker with his own fish-house left to him by his father, Mark Tether

Jinnie's Mum, Jane, had been unfortunate to be deserted by her husband, leaving her with two children but he would not give her a divorce and she had to carry his name, Forth, for the rest of her life. The same man went on to give his new woman ten children!

Jinnie's parents came together after her father's wife died leaving him with two little girls, living only a few doors away. and so they began to help each other and thus a friendship developed and blossomed, hence the partnership was established.

However as the years went by things were not as rosy as one

supposed and her father turned out to be one of those colourful characters one reads about. Apparently owning his own business had turned his head somewhat. So much so that he began spending, having a house built in front of the fish house and with a bathroom etc., with a shop frontage. He bought a very large car, a Maxwell with a chauffer no less. Jinnie had a pony and trap.

It was teatime and the men were on their way home from work. The horns and whistles were telling everyone this from the factories and docks, the fish houses and railroads, just across the road. The month was August and Jinnie welcomed the usual noises from the street outside, children demanding their teas, the sound of clogs on the pavement plus the horses and wagons on their way back to their stables.

Nurse Turpin turned to Grandma saying, " Go and see to your teas love while I make Jinnie comfortable."

Lizzie turned, promising the midwife a cup of tea. Not long after the midwife left, the baby was looking up into her Dad's eyes. "Well what do you think Jim?" His answer came back, "Isn't she small? I'm going to call her Tottie.".

So began my journey like many before me, born into this bustling world of streets, shops, beer-offs, public houses, public baths, sellers shouting their wares from handcarts, ships horns blasting from the docks just minutes away across the railway tracks, where trains were shunting wagons all through the night.

My own earliest memories that I can recall are when I was three years old and I was taken by Mrs Cass, who I found later had kept in touch with my mother. I remember being in this house with the lady who had a garden with a large dog with puppies and they turned out to be my playmates, so I was to spend most of my time inside the kennel with the furry puppies.

When I returned home I was to find that I had a baby brother so I must have been three years old.

It has surprised me that these memories can stay with me all through one's lifetime, so clear with every detail and I must admit that I enjoy being able to pass on these words to my family to follow.

The next memory has always without fail appeared to me so clearly that I must share it.

Living in these streets on Hessle Road, these communities

were so close, that the children felt safe no matter what. On one particular errand, being five years old, I was to encounter, standing before me as I turned the street corner, my eyes staring on the ground at a very large pair of feet. They never moved so my eyes turned skywards until I saw a pair of very big hands holding a tray with things hanging down from it. My eyes continued looking up to see the biggest smile looking down at me with large eyes set in a black man's face. To this day it brings a smile to my face because it gave me such a lovely surprise, tiny me meeting my first black person and he lights up my face whenever I remember him. Where I am concerned, colour, whatever it may be, white, red, pink, yellow, brown, black, all I feel is that everyone can and should get a long together. If only.

I was brought up in Wassand Street, living with loving parents in a house at the back of Mr Foster's shop being used as storeroom. It was on the corner of terrace. I remember Mam doing washing in the yard in a dolly tub and the clothes being hung out on lines across the terrace. I also remember the aunties and grannies doing net braiding outside the fronts of their houses. The youngsters were allowed the freedom of the street, as every mother knew that other mothers would take care of them.

I remember my Dad, Jim breeding canaries in the attic. They were one of the few luxuries that people could afford in those days. In the summer you could hear them singing outside their houses, hanging in cages on the walls.

There were lots of cats to keep the mice and rats down, I remember.

Across the street lived my Grandma Forth (Jane) and Uncle Jack with Aunt Eva and my cousins George, Norman and Cyril living close by Grandma Hookam and their family. Really they were friends of Mam and Dad's but in the streets it was not unusual for non-relatives to call the elderly, Aunty or Granddad. I suppose that it went along as a sign of friendship and respect within a community all closely linked to the fishing industry.

As most children are in their early years , we were oblivious to the scarcity of everything in most homes.

I remember still having to go to the corner shop for a gas mantle. It was so fragile, much like a white cobweb held together with chalk. It was put into a paper bag with the shopkeeper telling you how to hold it.

Another thing has just come to mind as I recall there was the wireless that had a very heavy battery that had to be taken to Mr Sheard's shop at the top of the street next to the pawnshop. Mr Sheard had a bicycle repair shop and he used to repair or charge the battery. He also used to sell fireworks for bonfire night, which was held on the road in the middle of the streets with piles of wood from fish boxes. There would be four or five different bonfires down the centre of the streets with the parents, uncles and aunts sitting outside their houses on stools and chairs. Fireworks came mainly in the order of hand held sparklers. Then the fun would start when the fire engines would appear to put out the fires, understandably.

The famous pawnshop on Hessle Road corner, at the top of the street was used by the fisherman's wives, quite often, to keep them going, after their men had left for the fishing grounds in the north. Most of the men had a decent suit that was kept for his few days, two or three at the most, on shore. As soon as they knew that he had left the dock, the suit would be parcelled up and taken to the pawnshop, in exchange for a few coppers to help the wives reach the next payday. Then a sigh of relief would go round when they knew that the ship did not have to return with engine trouble, seeing as their men never knew about this arrangement with the owner of the shop. When things got really desperate, it was not unknown for bowls of dough to be pawned for a day, allowing them to rise before they were retrieved at the end of the day with a payment of a farthing or a halfpenny for the service.

When I was roughly six years old I remember that our little family moved from the back of the shop to live with my Dad's parents and Uncle Harold, at the other end of Wassand Street, number 100, to look after Grandma Hodgson who was poorly. I thought that it was good because for the first time we had a front door and my brother Bill and me, slept in the attic where I eventually learned how to open the roof window by standing on a chair, where the whole world opened up to me. . I have never forgotten that moment when I first opened that window. I could see way over the rail yards, way over to the River Humber and at the other sides were the fields of Lincolnshire. It was my secret because I knew that I shouldn't have done it.. We were now only a few doors from my other cousins and I was allowed to go to Langham picture house on Hessle Road. It was round about the time that I felt that everything was becoming different because I had now started at Constable Street School, on the opposite side of Hessle Road, where a jolly policeman would take us all across the road and across the tram lines where we would all go past the famous Boyes shop on our way to school.

Our next move, I believe, was when I was six or seven and I was to experience a very different life style. This move was a very big surprise. It turned out to be a long way away, past Pickering Park on the borders of Hessle. The grandparents went with us where we found ourselves looking across at fields, hedges and at the back we could see allotments, with things growing. It was Dad who did all of the talking because as usual Mam was too busy with our new brother Jim, who all of the relatives called Tim!

We now had a bathroom, no more tin bath in front of the fire. We had a garden front and back and our house had a name above the door, it was called 'The Nook". This was around the years 1935 to 1936.

Two houses along from ours was a small lane, I think that it was called Lynton Avenue, with a few houses and right at the end was a bungalow and a small lake where anglers used to fish. It was some months before I discovered this. Much to my surprise, I was to be introduced to my new school, Pickering Road, where the trod to the allotments ran into it. I remember Dad taking me to see his allotment just at the back of our house. It was to be my first introduction to plant life and other things that live off the plants and under the soil. It has never left me, this fascination, for plants and all other living matter.

Time moves on and seeing brother Bill now age five coming to school with myself. I now had a bike so Bill sat on the seat, with me standing on the pedals and when it rained Bill held an umbrella to keep us dry.

As time went by the Grandparents were becoming very unhappy. They missed the usual things they'd had in Wassand Street. Also Mam was finding things much harder financially and so one day Dad asked me if I wanted to go back and I surprised him with the answer, "well we had Langham and the swimming baths and Hessle Road shops and our cousins there didn't we?". He just looked sad and said, "I suppose you're right". In the meantime plans had already been made and we, with the Grandparents came back to Hessle Road. Wellstead Street was our new address and I was back at my first school Constable Street, which was only a few yards away at the end of the street.

So we went on looking after the Grandparents until after a long illness we lost Granddad. I don't really remember being at the funeral. I came to realise that as children, we were always looked after by aunts and friends of our parents during those occasions.

THE WAR AND EVACUATION

We were now seeing changes beginning to happen. As the young 'uns we were always in the dark about future events so we only went along, 'just one day at a ' visiting Langham and watching Tom Mix on the screen and exchanging sweets. Then we began to notice that all of the adults were talking about the same things and became inquisitive. It was something to do with Germany and Hitler, so then we began to question Mams and Dads.

This was 1939 and then they had to start to tell us about certain things changing and in no time at all the cats were out of the bag and evacuation was starting to be discussed. It was at that time that we all began to listen to the radio and began to understand as only children do and in their own way it sounded just like a film. The lads started playing at war.

The parents had to tell them the truth about evacuation and why it had to be. It was now beginning to sound more like a holiday to all of the youngsters. A train ride with some of your pals just for a while because you would be coming home again. I remember it being announced on the radio, the date for this evacuation and shouted it out to Mam who was in the yard with the washing. I remember her dashing to the radio and she didn't look very pleased so I went out to my friends. Then began the preparation for the days to come and our parents signed the forms for Bill and myself to be kept together. This was not to be.

Bill and me were in school, and I remember looking up to see Mam stood in the classroom door with a funny look I had never seen before. Then we were soon with our teachers, boarding a train, with them telling us that everything was going to be fine. I don't remember any tears and we were all too busy looking in our carrier bags, doing 'swaps' with the biscuits etc. that were inside. We all felt that it was like a holiday.

Bill didn't leave until later, he was only eight years old and in floods of tears and apparently Mam took some consoling but she had Jim to see to at home who was only four years old. Little did Bill and me realise that we were going in different directions.

Unfortunately as Mam received two postcards, one from Dunnington near York, from Bill and mine from Scarborough!

Mam was so distressed that Dad borrowed a bike during the next two weekends and biked to Scarborough to make sure that I was O.K. and then followed the next one biking to Dunnington to see Bill.

As it so happened I wrote home asking why I couldn't go to my brother Bill and the next thing I knew Mam had arranged for us both to be together.

I was living in a large house at the end of a crescent shaped avenue . The house was called 'Childhaven'. It had previously been used for poor mums and children to have free holidays. It still remains today and is now a children's nursery bearing the same name, Childhaven.

Mam arrived at the house one evening in the middle of bath time. Imagine a small classroom of girls being lined up to take their baths. I finished up having a bath, then finding Mam darning the youngsters socks in the centre of all us children in the large kitchen. After saying our goodbyes to my friends and teachers who were called, Miss Bun and Miss Smithson, who had looked after us , we set off for a relatives house in Scarborough to spend the night there and the next morning we boarded the bus to York. When we left the bus at Kexby Crossing we then had roughly a mile to walk to the village of Dunnington, which was to be my home, with my brother for the next two and a half years. Bill stayed on until the war ended.

As we approached the village green I saw my brother holding a ladies hand coming towards us. This lady had taken Bill in and

LIFE IS WHAT YOU MAKE IT

now myself. After saying our hello's we set off to the house and I now had a comfortable feeling about this lady who insisted upon being called by her Christian name which was Dolly, which I felt even more comfortable with.

After Mam had left for home, Doll began to make me more at home. We lived in a modern house in School Lane that had been built onto a corner shop owned by a Miss Bails and her father.

Our water supply came from a well which was situated in between our two front doors and all there was to be seen above ground was an old village pump.

Being together with brother Bill made things much easier being introduced to country life, the farms and animals and the village school just across the lane. Not forgetting Doll's husband, really called Jack Everest but everyone called him Toddy. So we settled down with Doll and Toddy who had no children of their own.

It turned out that we were living with an ex professional footballer, Toddy* and Doll was the village bookie if you wanted to place a bet.

* **John "Jack" Everest** (born 20 July 1908) was an Irish former professional footballer. During his career, he made over 100 appearances in the Football League.

After beginning his career with non-league sides Dunnington and Heslington, Everest turned professional with York City in 1926 before joining Stockport County in 1928, scoring seven goals in seven matches for the *Hatters* including four during a 7–1 victory over Carlisle United on 18 January 1930. Originally playing as a forward, he converted to playing as a defender in 1931 while playing for Blackpool. Everest joined Cardiff City in 1934 following a recommendation from George Blackburn, who had seen Everest play against his Cheltenham Town side in the FA Cup. He was ever present in his debut season at Ninian Park, playing in each of the club's 47 matches in all competitions and remained first choice the following season, but with the club finishing in 19th and 20th position in his two seasons, Everest was one of a number of players released by manager Ben Watts-Jones in an attempt to improve the club's standings. He later played for Southend United and

Joyce Chatwin

Barnsley.
Scource: Wikipedia

As time went on we just became oblivious to the fact that we were at war with anyone and Doll always turned the radio off when we kids were in the house during news time. Letters were being sent home by myself but in Mum's letters she never put anything in about the war.

So there we both were roaming around the countryside and we were in another world, learning about farm animals and growing things. Of course there were other evacuees, from our own town even, from the streets that we knew.

School days were very different as the numbers of evacuees and teachers amounted to many more than was usual in a village school. Other arrangements had to be made as to where we would all fit in. As there were only classrooms in the school, the back room in the village chapel and the Reading Room were used for mornings and afternoons. It worked quite well actually.

Some of the school holidays were spent on the farms when we were old enough, about twelve yrs. old, to help with the harvests. Sometimes we were allowed extra time off school for this and our pay was five shillings a day.

Toddy had built a pigsty at the back of the garden and so we now had two young pigs that we treated like pets.

One of my favourite places of interest was a small farm on York Street owned by Mr Buckle who was a widower I believe. The household was made up of two sons, two daughters and Aunt Lill.

Aunt Lill took care of the dairy where she taught me how to separate the cream from the milk with which she also taught me to make butter and when calving time arrived, she taught me how to feed the calves, which I often did.

They had two horses for the heavy work, one called Violette.

One day I went to call and Aunt Lill said to me that there was a surprise down the yard but that I mustn't open the stable door.

I did what she said but the top half of the door was open a crack so I peeped over the door to see that the mare had a young foal. He was beautiful and we called him Prince.

The winters during the war were, I think, some of the worst I remember. Toddy had to move the snow at the back door, which was up to the top. There were huge icicles and beautiful frost patterns on the windows.

All of us youngsters were sledging and sliding and I remember going to the wood, which was made up with lots of conifers, to bring barrow loads of fir cones with which Doll made the fire. We were up to our knees in them but to us it was all good fun.

The school was Church of England and so Sundays meant morning services and afternoon Sunday school.

The Archbishop of York confirmed Brother Bill and myself during our stay in Dunnington.

All the while the war was being fought and the Germans and ourselves were bombing one another and unbeknown to Bill and me Doll and Toddy were about to give a home to our brother Jim who was five and a half years old. We were to find out later the circumstances that caused Mam to part with her youngest son. Apparently there had been a lot of bombing on Hull during that time and Mam had thrown herself over Jim in the air raid shelter to save him when the blast from the bomb went into Mam's face, as she was near the entrance. She lost her voice completely for a week or more and she knew that she had to get brother Jim out of Hull. So one day to our surprise, after school, there was a little brother Jim sat in the kitchen. It must have been an awful time for him but Mam and Dad wanted him to be safe with us in the country.

Throughout the process of writing this book I have spoken with members of my family to sharpen accounts of our family history and ensure that what I have written is as accurate as possible and on one of these occasions my brothers, Jim and Bill gave me their version of their time in Dunnington as evacuees.

" At the very tender age of six years, I actually volunteered to go the village of Dunnington, near York, for the duration of World War 11. For safety from the bombings on Hull.

My brother William and my sister Joyce were already away from the family home for the same reason. Looking back on this arrangement, it seems almost incredible that such a little boy should climb into a truck, driven by a distant relative and dropped off at the front door, saying goodbye to my Mum and Dad for a totally unknown future!

I blended in with the village people, the church, and the school and even joined the church choir managing to sing a few solos. I extended my love for music and singing with trips to the local public house to entertain the local drinkers. Much to the chagrin of the church organist (who was also my head teacher at my school.

I realise now that I must have had a great deal of confidence but some of this confidence was supported by my elder brother Bill, who acted as my bodyguard and kept me from harm, for which I will be ever grateful.

My childhood, on the whole was happy and we all had space in that countryside to play in, for many, many hours.

As a small child my maturity was formed by being exposed to animals, rough farmhand drunks, who occasionally could be violent. I witnessed horses at stud, the local bull servicing many young heifers in one afternoon, to the cheering of the local farmhands and being present and assisting in slaughtering pigs and watching the local butcher dismember them in front of our very eyes. And all of this became the norm.

In short, it was a young life of a boy gradually being strengthened for the needs of the future man and looking back, it has served me well.

I will finish on a risqué note - THE ARRIVAL OF THE LAND ARMY GIRLS!

The ladies of the soil used to tease us young lads in the fields where we were working. My memories of that are graphic and completed (almost) our education on biology and all before I was eleven years old."

James (Jim) Hodgson

"On my arrival at Dunnington at the young age of 8 years, I had to sleep in a cot for the first few weeks before I was moved to Doll and Toddy's, to be cared for , during the rest of the war. I became a choirboy and was confirmed in Dunnington Church.

After returning home aged 14 years, I became a factory worker at Smith and Nephews. My next place of work was a cabin boy aboard one of Hull's fishing trawlers. Trawling in the

Arctic in the winter months was no fun. I went overboard during one trip and was picked up ten minutes later from the freezing water. Another accident happened, leaving me with a broken jaw. In the end, I did however gain my Skipper's Ticket and sailed as the captain in a number of trawlers from the Hull fleet.

I have to face the fact that when I left the sea behind me, I was an alcoholic, an illness that was so common amongst fishermen due to the harsh lifestyle, including spending so much time away from my family. With the help of my family and particularly my wife, Betty and Alcoholics Anonymous, I have remained free from drink for many, many years now.

Betty has been by my side ever since attending and helping at the 'AA' meetings, even running 'ALANON', which supports the families of those afflicted with this terrible curse.

Betty has been my anchor, all the way through, God Bless Her."

William (Bill) Hodgson

By 1942, I had reached the age of thirteen and a half and I was asked by my parents if I would be willing to go home to go to a private college and so as the war years progressed I returned to Hull to meet new friends from the college.

I returned to Dunnington many times over the years, even taking my boyfriend, Ken, who my brothers Bill and Jim, took too instantly.

In between college I found myself work in a fish merchants office on St Andrews Dock.

I went for the interview to find the office was up above the fish market. This really was no surprise to me, belonging to the 'fishy folk' of Hessle Road. You must remember that my views from the window of my office looked down on the roof covering the top of the fish market and so I became used to giant seagulls landing on the window sill and in winter, with darkness falling earlier and a lack of outside lighting, due to the blackout regulations, I often looked from my typewriter to see an audience of large rats on the window ledge. I became used to them and amused by them.

When at the age of 15 I met my future husband, Ken, who was taken into the forces when he reached 18 yrs. The war with

Germany had just finished but there was much to be settled over there.. He was to serve nearly three years in the R.A.F. Regiment, mostly in Germany and was asked to stay on for training in England. His reply was, 'No, I just want to get home to my wife', as we were married on 20th September 1947 at St Barnabus Church, Boulevard, Hessle Road, Hull. The date had been set but nothing was heard from Germany, forcing me to approach our vicar and it was due to him that Ken was granted leave.

That very same vicar we all said was a hero because during the air raids he would go from shelter to shelter along Boulevard, trying to keep his people in good spirits.

Ken had become a part of the family as soon as he was introduced. We agreed to come together on New Years Eve at a dance held in Madeley Street, where a wooden dance floor covered the swimming baths.

The war continued to rule everyone's lives but I must admit the fact that for most teenagers we had only a sense of blotting it out as much as possible. Even though we were still using the air raid shelters with Mam having to wake us up when the sirens went and me climbing back into bed on the opposite side! I never got away with it though. Dad was still working at the fish smoke houses and he would be at night on fire duty on the roof. We mustn't forget that the factories and other important buildings had to be guarded during the air raids. My cousin George, who was sixteen, had to go from one Air Raid Patrol (ARP) Station to others taking messages on his bike.

Of course the discussions between us all would be music and what pictures where on at the cinema and the latest dances, especially when the Boogie arrived.

Sometimes the sirens would blow during a picture show and it would come up on the screen for us to go to safety. I remember when I was at college on Anlaby Road and we all had to go to the shelters in the garden.

My Mam, Jinnie, was leaving her work at the shop, it was a 'beer off'', one night at ten o'clock . It was pitch black and she had to find her way from Fosters shop in Wassand Street, along Goulton Street, known locally as Bank End, to get home to Boulevard. She told me that she was holding onto house walls eventually arriving home safely. The following day she discovered that she had miraculously just missed falling into a large bomb crater , which had been intended for the rail yards just a few yards away.

Eventually the war came to end but not before Hull was battered heavily by the German bombs, being one of the worst blitzed cities in the U.K. Although it was reportedly the second worst bombed city in England, London being the first, it was rarely named in any news reports and referred to only as, 'a City on the east coast', maybe for security reasons.

After the street parties and parades to celebrate the end of World War 11, the city and it's folk slowly returned to some kind of normality. Bombed buildings and streets became the playground for the kids and it was no exception along Hessle Road.

During the war, many of the trawlers sailing out of Hull had been requisitioned by the Navy and with the addition of a few small guns; they became mine and submarine sweepers. Many more lives were lost but at the cessation of the war the fishing industry began to re-build and Hull became one of the biggest and most important fishing ports in Britain and Europe.

KEN CHATWIN AND HIS FAMILY

His family lived in the next street to our own. A larger family than ours and I will now introduce my in-laws, Clara and Jack and their family.

Father - John (Jack) William Chatwin
Mother - Clara Elizabeth Chatwin
Children - John (died aged 3) Clara Jnr., Jack, Harry, Dorothy, Sidney, Kenneth and Thelma - plus three miscarriages.

Although this book was prompted by photographs and stories from Jane Forth's album and travels through the history of the Tethers and Hodgsons i.e. my side of the family, I must include my husband's family history. There are no photographs before Ken's mother and father's generation and the oldest that we have is of Jack Chatwin as a young soldier in the 1st World War.

We do however have a small amount of documentation from Ken's Grandfather, Henry Chatwin's past, and it tells a very interesting story.

Henry Chatwin spent thirteen years of his life as a Private in

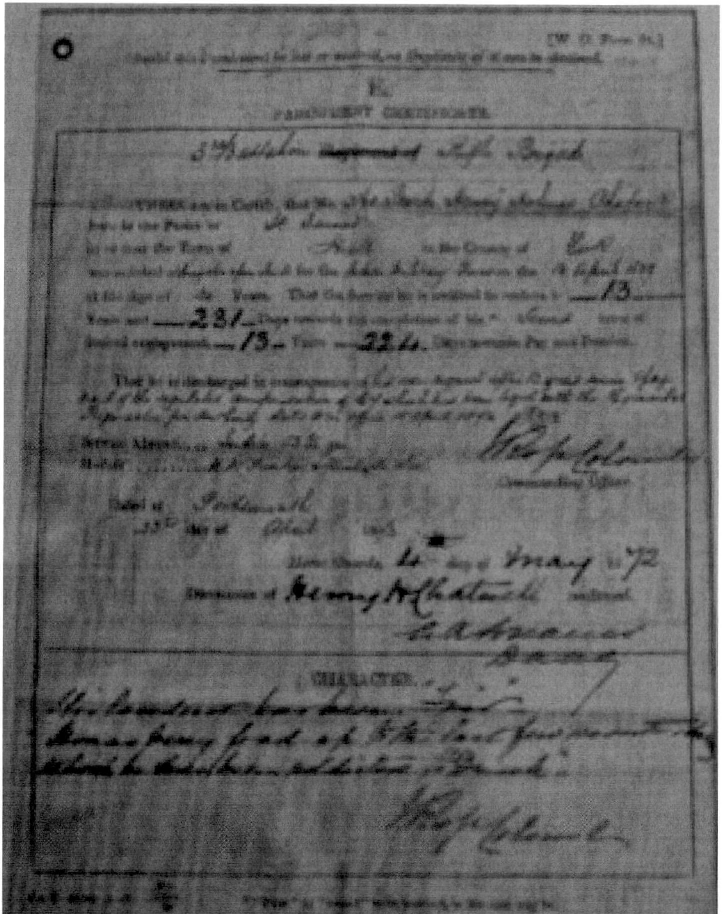

Henry Chatwin's discharge papers

LIFE IS WHAT YOU MAKE IT

the 3rd Battalion, Rifle Brigade, in India from 1859 to the day of his discharge on 4th May 1872. We know this from his Discharge papers, which still exist in remarkably good condition.

The information on the papers tells more than just his personal details and dates and a great deal about life in the British Army, in India during the start of the period known as the 'British Raj', as Britain under Queen Victoria's Monarchy expanded the Commonwealth.

As this period began in 1858, Henry Chatwin arrived in India, just as one of the most significant periods of British history began.

*'The **history of the British Raj** refers to the period of British rule on the Indian subcontinent between 1858 and 1947. The system of governance was instituted in 1858 when the rule of the East India Company was transferred to the Crown in the person of Queen Victoria (who in 1876 was proclaimed Empress of India).' Wikipedia*

The paper also tells us that Henry was discharged as a 'consequence of his own request', which was possibly not completely true as it also describes his 'Character' thus , 'His Conduct has been "Fair"... Being good up to the last few months in which he has become addicted to Drink'.

This means that this discharge was a 'Doolally Tap'.

The dictionary defines this condition as,

'From Deolali (the name of a former British army camp 100 miles north-east of Bombay, used as a transit station for soldiers awaiting transport back to Britain) + tap (from Persian or Urdu ??? (tab, "malarial fever"), ultimately from Sanskrit ???(t?pa, "heat; fever")).' Wikipedia

From this comes the term for 'madness' as doolaly, which is commonly used today as a slang term in the English language.

The next document, another Certificate of Discharge, is from 25th February 1888 but this time it is Henry's discharge from a fishing smack, the SS Witham. Fishing Smacks were traditional fishing boats, which in Henry's time aboard would have fished under sail. Some Smacks were later fitted with coal-powered steam engines.

Sadly, research shows that the SS Witham was "shelled and sunk in the North Sea on 18th April, 1917 by a vessel of the

Henry Chatwin's discharge papers from the Fishing Smack SS Witham

Imperial German Navy," but thankfully, "Her crew survived."

The document tells us that the SS Witham sailed out of Boston and was 'Trawling the North Sea' and that Henry's, 'Character for Ability' was Very Good as was his 'Certificate for Conduct.

There is very little else known about the generations of Chatwin's, before Henry and in fact little more known about Ken's Grandparent's lives.

Ken's Grandma on his father's side, having lost her husband (Henry), took in washing to feed her two boys and this unfortunate lady was stone deaf. She was fortunate in a sense that Clara, Ken's mother, was her neighbour.

Ken's mum Clara, born on the 21st December 1889, came from a family of eight. Clara's father, Bob King, came to Hull from the south, looking for work among our fishing fleet of Smacks.

Young Kenneth's life differed from mine in as much that his Mam and Dad finished up with a much larger family, bringing much more hardship for everyone as the family numbered nine in all with the deaths of three new-born along the way.

After they were married many sad events clouded the horizon for the couple. Their first-born son was taken ill and died at the age of two with pneumonia. Before the death of the little boy, a little girl was born.

Clara and Jack had seven children and three miscarriages before Ken appeared on the scene and his arrival was in very poor circumstances.

On 20th February 1928, a baby boy was born to Clara Chatwin and the address was the Old Workhouse at the back of the Hull Infirmary, where Clara had been admitted by her doctor, feeling that she was at risk having in the past a history of seriously damaging labours – losing three babies in the process.

The doctors therefore had no choice but to place Clara in the charity hospital for the safety of mother and child. She was placed here as she was just one of many working class Mothers who could not afford to pay hospital fees. He was given the name Kenneth.

In the meantime Jack was taken from his trade as a sawyer to be part of our army, on it's way to the trenches, in the First World

Joyce Chatwin

Left:
Ken Chatwin Snr as a baby,
held by his eldest sister Clara

Below left:
John (Jack) William Chatwin
as a young soldier

Below:
Ken Chatwin in his RAF Uniform

LIFE IS WHAT YOU MAKE IT

War. During his time in the war, he was gassed and wounded many times. When he returned home, he had no sense of smell and still had shrapnel in his leg and a drop foot, for which he received a pension, it being the grand total of ten shillings per week.

One day a policeman delivered a telegram to Clara to announce that her husband had been killed in action and from oral family history, he had been gassed in a shell hole and after his troop had moved on, he came round and had to walk for a long time before he found other Englishmen.

No one informed the grieving family and some time later he turned up at the house, unannounced.

Ken often described his impoverished upbringing as 'Dickensian' and sometimes the terrible health conditions in the cramped housing and a lack of NHS care and treatment led to quite astonishing procedures. Ken had a large feather shaped scar on his back, that he used to tell the children was caused by a German bayonet. The truth was probably more horrific. When a very young child a doctor operated on him on the kitchen table, which one doctor later in his life said that it was a typical scar from an operation to remove a Tuberculosis cyst. His brother, Syd had spent a long time in a special hospital with tuberculosis.

As mentioned earlier, Ken, like his Dad was conscripted into the armed forces but just after WW11 had ended. He was part of the R.A.F. Regiment and was to be part of the clear up operation in Germany and always said that he hated almost every moment of forces' life.

He would tell me about his time in Germany, having gone through the bombing at home, he now had to endure the plight of the women and children across in Germany. He told me, as they travelled towards their destination, they were to witness town after town raised to the ground with not a building standing. His words were, "you think rationing at our side is bad, think yourselves lucky because we saw them coming out of cellars and having to barter what little they had left, going miles into the countryside".

I never forgot the story that he told me about the night that he was on guard duty at the gates of the prisoner of war camp. It was Christmas time and the Germans, like ourselves had terrible

Joyce Chatwin

Our Wedding Day, 20th September 1947
at St Barnabas Church, Hull

gales and snow. Ken went on to surprise me with what he was to witness on that dark winter's night.

He spotted a figure, some distance away trudging through the snow, approaching the gates and realized that it was an old lady covered in snow. It appeared that she was trying to get permission to see her husband, who was a German officer being held prisoner in the camp. She was eventually allowed her request. Ken got his buddies to leave the hut for the old lady to get warm and so she was to enjoy seeing her husband, between two guards naturally, but they were allowed some privacy in the hut and when she left, the officer couldn't thank our soldiers enough for how they had treated his wife, as they had all given her their own food.

The truth was that Ken hated his time in the forces and being away from home for such long periods but he did develop a real compassion for the German people, which lasted for the rest of his life. He also managed to find some things that he could enjoy such as being part of a gymnastics team that gave displays at various events and ceremonies.

As with many of the family Ken had a good singing voice and perhaps his greatest claim to fame, which certainly became a famous family story, was winning an armed forces singing competition, culminating in a performance with a Forces Big Band in a stadium in Hamburg and the offer of a recording contract. But this would mean that he would have to prolong his time away from home and he turned down the offer of possible fame and fortune and returned home as soon as he could, to start his own family life. In fact Ken was so keen to start his family life that he came home to marry me before he was officially demobbed. He had to request a special leave to get married and I had to visit our vicar to request that he write to Ken's commanding officer making the request official and genuine.

So Ken returned home and the wedding day arrived on 20th September 1947. Unfortunately we woke to pouring rain but nothing was going to stop the ceremony and as we arrived at St Barnabas Church, at the top of South Boulevard, now sadly demolished, the sun came out and the wedding went off almost without a hitch. It seemed that towards the end of the ceremony, we were being hurried along and we had the photographs taken

Joyce Chatwin

Jane, Jinnie and me - three generations of remarkable women

on the grass at the back of the church. We only learned later, from the florist who had a shop across Hessle Road that there were so many people who wanted to attend the ceremony, they spilled out onto Hessle Road, stopping the traffic. This delayed the next wedding party and hence the 'hurry up' at the end.

We had our honeymoon in Withernsea, before Ken had to return to Germany, as his demob was put back due to a scare with the Russians making noises with the rest of the allies, that they were not happy with the way Germany was being divided up after the war. Thankfully it didn't come to anything, except that some say it started the 'Cold War'.

Anyway, Ken was eventually demobbed and he returned home to start married life and return to his job as a filleter on the fish dock. He was an extremely hard working man and at times had more than one job to earn enough money to ensure that his children would not have to endure a childhood like the one that he had. With my support and hard work we eventually moved to our own house in Hessle, which raised a few eyebrows down Hessle Road as we were considered to be going 'posh'.

Sadly Jack Chatwin, Ken's dad, died at home in 1966, in Eton Street, probably his injuries from his time at war contributed to his demise and the last thing that he asked for was that his son, Ken, gave him a shave, to make him 'look right'. Ken's mother Clara survived Jack by another eight years but after a series of illnesses, she sadly died on 2nd October 1979 at the age of ninety. She had a stroke which caused her to collapse behind the front door of 30 Eton Street, the same house that Jack ended his days in.

After the collapse of the fishing industry in Hull and having to sell his, 'fish round' he looked for work in various factories, which he found, but after being made redundant more than once, he decided to retire and made an adventurous decision to move to the Isle of Skye.

Eventually moving back to Hull and after a few other jobs he actually retired when the rigours of his working life began to affect his health. Another move saw them sell their house and move into council accommodation, in a sheltered housing bungalow.

Finally they moved to Cherry Burton with daughter Jenny and

Joyce Chatwin

Jack and Clara Chatwin
enjoying the 'good times'

Ken Chatwin
20th February 1928
to 14th January 2014

after a few very happy years he passed away peacefully on 14th January 2014.

His life was aptly summed up in the eulogy that his family wrote and had printed for the many people who attended his funeral. Here are some extracts;

" Ken had a great sense of humour which he bestowed on his family.

He loved talking and telling stories, especially about his days down Hessle Road and his working life on the fish dock, where we learned of such characters as Ginger Mink, Bob Armstrong and Ted Rutter.

Ken was an honest man and would never compromise on his principles.

He had strong standards and favourite phrases such as, "if you leave this house looking like that, then don't think about coming back".... commenting on his offspring's fashion choices.

"I wish I had your head full of threepenny bits," if you got too big for your boots.

"What you need is an aspirin, an early night and a haircut," to cure all ills.

KEN'S LEGACY

Ken Chatwin loved life and particularly family life. He worked in very tough jobs, often with three jobs at once, to make sure that he and I could provide the best for our family. Our first house - owned not rented - was a proud step forward and we made sure that the kids went short of nothing.

He owned a fish and chip shop and a fish round.

Following a move to a new address in Hessle, Ken and I moved to the Isle of Skye. We then moved back down to Hull, in the late eighties, after our Scottish island adventure.

Ken loved music: Sinatra, Bennett, Fitzgerald and Vaughan, The Big Bands: Basie, Ellington, Dorsey... and Brass Bands

He loved Westerns and War films: True Grit, The Alamo, The Quiet Man, John Wayne, Gary Cooper, James Stewart.....

Ken also loved holidays and travelling: Filey, Brid and Scarborough, Scotland, Spain, Yugoslavia, Austria and perhaps his favourite of all, Germany and the Black Forest.

He bought a boat.

Joyce Chatwin

Ken loved food: beef, greens, kippers, cooked breakfasts with smoked haddock and tomato gravy, savaloys. He loved fish: chat haddocks, skate, plaice and crabs, coconut pies, curd cheese cake and custard tarts.

Ken loved sport: Football, Manchester United and Hull City. Rugby League, Hull F.C.... Snooker, darts cricket and most other sports that you would care to mention.

He loved his Daily Mirror.

PART 4

The Fourth Generation KEN, BILL, MARK & JENNY CHATWIN

In 1949, our first son, Kenneth James, was born at home after a long labour, having to be brought into the world with the use of forceps. We were both very lucky to have Dr Dunn and Dr Heap and a midwife, who was the daughter of the famous Hessle Road midwife, Nurse Turpin, who brought me into the world!

Happiness reined at our house with a new baby and meantime across the road at Grandma's house we see Grandma trying to look after her daughter Eva who lay very ill with cancer. She insisted to Grandma that she wanted to see me and the baby. As soon as I was well enough I paid her a visit with our baby, to hear her saying that she wanted me to have her rented house. I was choking back my tears at the same time to witness Aunt Eva thinking of me while she lay dying. I never forgot that day. She passed away very soon after that and so Ken and me and our son, had to make preparations to move into Carlton Terrace in South Boulevard, our first home.

The year was 1949 and many happy days were spent there before young Kenny now aged two became very ill with meningitis. Very little was known about this disease at the time but after six traumatic weeks in hospital, where we were not allowed to see him except from behind a curtained window, you may be able to feel the joy in having him back home. I remember going to confirmation during that awful time as it appeared to me that our son had lived through two miracles, the first being born and now this. So we leave 1951 to face many other sad events with Ken's work etc.

Through his lifetime we seemed to sail along, myself doing part time office work, then Metal Box for three months. One day Ken asked me if I would mind if he tried casual bobbing. It's a funny term I know but really it was a well known expression amongst Hessle Road folk. Bobbers were the men who worked through the night, unloading fish from the trawler's hold onto the market. It involved, 'below men loading fish into baskets, winch men lifting the baskets up above deck, swingers to swing the baskets and weighmen to catch and weigh out the fish into ten stone kits.' So he became a bobber.

In the meantime, on 10th January 1954, I gave Ken another son, William John, who weighed in at 10lbs. Ken's Mam Clara was there to help and she was always happy to do it. He was christened at the Fishermen's Chapel on Bank End (Goulton Street), named after his Uncle Bill who was a trawler man and who became his godfather.

We had now moved into a larger house nearer to Mam's at 365, South Boulevard and as time went by Ken became a fully-fledged bobber.

In 1956, our third son appeared on the scene. Another 10lb bouncing boy, named Mark Stephen after his Great, Great Grandfather Mark Tether who had set up his own business, fish smoking early in the 1900s.

It had reached a point in time, now having three children, that we should be thinking about their futures and so we began to make plans, which was to give ourselves a year for banking enough for a deposit on a house. Ken asked, 'How?'

The plan was, that all my wages and Ken's extra money that he earned in part-time jobs, went into the bank. He began to laugh at me until I said that I told him that nothing will be wasted. Where food and clothing was concerned I would be making bread and any clothing and making the most of other foods. Grandma's sewing machine was put to use.

Yes, that year was indeed very hard but in the year 1957 we moved into our own house at 2 St John's Walk, Hessle and at last we had a garden and a good school for the boys.

As the years came and went, there were more good and bad

memories. I was still working part time at Smith and Nephews and Ken was bobbing and doing other part time jobs, in building and window cleaning.

Surprise, surprise, we looked on as Ken decided to open a Fish and Chip shop on Gisburn Road, just round the corner from our house. It was to be open at lunchtimes and evenings, in between his nighttime bobbing.

Unfortunately , the price of fish began to rise on account of the trouble with Iceland introducing fishing exclusion limits which resulted in a series of conflicts known as 'The Cod Wars'. This eventually saw the demise of the fishing industry in Hull and the closure of St Andrew's Dock, which had once been the biggest fishing port in Europe. Many small fish businesses were affected financially and after a year he closed the shop. Ken, later had the offer to buy a small fish business, including a large van, which was a travelling fresh fish shop, selling mainly to farms and villages between Hull and the East Coast. This meant another house move, to 43 Cottesmore Road, Hessle to accommodate a garage large enough for the fish van and a large fridge.

On 24th April 1965, our daughter, who we named Jenny after my mother, arrived. She was the only one of our children to be born in hospital because she was breach but she was our own little beauty.

Ken Jnr who was now fourteen, decided to try living aboard a trawler at sea on what was ironically called, a pleasure cruise, which lasted three weeks during the summer school holidays. His Uncle Bill, who was a trawler skipper himself by this time, arranged it with one of his friends who was also a skipper. After the trip, young Ken told of his experiences, then added that it wasn't for him. That certainly pleased us too.

Life went on as usual, now with a baby to care for. I had to forget about part-time work and I could spend a bit more time in my garden as well, especially in the summertime while being able to have the company of Jenny and neighbours children, her age, with paddling pools etc. It was a bit of heaven for me too.

As time moves on, we are now, after a few years, approaching a very unsettling time within the fishing industry regarding fishermen's rights and health and safety. Fishing was regarded as the most dangerous occupation in Britain, with many fishermen losing their lives or being seriously injured while out at sea.

It all erupted in the winter of 1968, when a terrible storm sank three of our trawlers along with 58 trawlermen. The names of the trawlers were, St Romanus, Kingston Peridot and Ross Cleveland.

It appeared at the time to be not believable to the people on Hessle Road, who had over the years suffered the loss of many of their fathers, grandfathers and sons.

On this occasion, one trawlerman's wife from Hessle Road began to thump the table in her kitchen shouting, 'Enough is enough,' to her daughter. Something had to be done and she vowed to do it. Her name was Lily Bilocca and she set about gathering her little band of fishermen's wives, fighting for the rights of their men.

Lily and three others along with John Prescott, who was then a union convener, travelled to the Houses of Parliament and only then were the safety regulations changed. Thanks to Lily Bilocca and her companions, new laws came into practice, the main one of which was that every trawler leaving for the fishing grounds had to have a trained radio operator on board, as well as the skipper. It was also enforced that a ship must be available, at all times, to support the fishing fleets, acting as a hospital ship with medical help to deal with the many illnesses and horrific injuries that often occurred at sea and so the wives had not only changed working and safety conditions for their menfolk but also history.

Unfortunately, in such a male dominated community, not all men took their wives actions with gratitude as 'women should not meddle in such matters.'

PART 5

THE STORIES

When the idea of turning my notes and short accounts of events, following the lives of three generations of my family, through a photograph album, into a book, I had to consider the limits that I should work within. These limits had to include, how far I should expand the 'family tree' branches from the main trunk. I knew that if I tried to include too many members of the family, I would never finish writing and the book would become unwieldy and of not much interest to anyone outside of the family. I therefore apologise to any family members who feel that their stories have been 'missed out'.

Another limit has been to try and imagine/gauge how much information is necessary to tell an accurate account of an event, while keeping it interesting for a wider audience of readers and I have therefore tried, wherever possible, to relate the lives and stories to national or international events to fix the moment in time to a bigger, perhaps more familiar historical timeline.

For instance, I find it fascinating that Jane Forth saw the real Buffalo Bill (William Cody), with his troupe, in Hull in the same decade that Billy the Kid (William Bonney), Wyatt Earp, Wild Bill Hicock and many other, now infamous characters from the ' Wild West' era of America, were alive and creating their part in that history. We, of course, a few generations on, became familiar with these people through Hollywood and the 'Cowboy' films that we saw in the cinemas.

Joyce Chatwin

To think that we have the actual documents, written on parchment, confirming significant events in the life of Henry Chatwin, as a soldier at the start of the Raj and as a seaman on sailing boats gives me a place in time to fix my family history.

But the most important 'limit' has been to decide when the main body of this story must end. After some discussion we decided that an appropriate place on the family's timeline, to draw matters to a close, is the end of Hull as a major fishing port and the demise of St Andrew's dock and of course Hessle Road as a community that ran through all of the lives of all of the members of our family.

Therefore the time limit that I have set begins in 1975, with the official closure of St Andrews Dock and ends in the mid 1980s as the streets on Hessle Road that I have written about began to be demolished and the Hessle roader's began to be dispersed across Hull.

I am however going to ask your indulgence to let me stray, slightly outside this boundary, in this section that I have named 'The Stories'.

Most of these accounts do fall well within the limits that I have set myself and I hope are interesting as part of general history but some of them tell my immediate family's tales almost up to the present day.

HEALTH, WELFARE AND SOCIAL CARE
The Means Test

Moving to a time in history, a miserable, never to be forgotten time when men were losing their jobs and the soup kitchens opened and these families were having to manage on even less.

The government decided to send inspectors round to assess if the Parish should give any help.

My parents had just finished paying for the piano, their only source of entertainment, 2 shillings and sixpence a week, for 2 years it had cost them. When the inspector gave them a visit he told them that they would have to sell the piano, as it was a luxury. They wouldn't and so they received no help.

The same order was given to young Kenneth's father, in their case it was the wireless set.

Young Ken witnessed this going on, seeing his father with his head in his hands. That wireless had helped to keep the family's spirit's up. He never forgot this unjust act and it guided his politics from that day to his last.

Health and Social Care

We now see these youngsters experiencing and beginning to accept changes taking place, for instance my grandmother had a nervous breakdown, making it necessary for my parents and youngsters to move in with grandparents. This turned out to be quite an ordeal as two uncles already lived there, swelling the numbers to six adults and three youngsters. This was to go on for quite some time until Jinnie collapsed through sheer exhaustion. Both the Hodgson and the Chatwin families and their pre-decessors suffered with serious health and welfare issues and before the National Health Service was put in place, there were often times when medical help was desperately needed but there was no money to pay for it.

On the occasion that Ken Snr had to be operated on, on the kitchen table, the doctor knew that the family could not afford the hospital fees and so chose to do the operation in the home, relying on the women from the street to clean and sterilize the room and table, as best they could.

Common childhood ailments, some with more serious consequences than others included; measles (which left Joyce and her brother with perforated eardrums), chickenpox, diphtheria, scarleteena, tuberculosis, scarlet fever, scabies, whooping cough, rickets, meningitis (which Ken Jnr survived) and many more that we don't hear of now.

Medicine was expensive and often difficult to come by and so homemade remedies were used such as standing children with chest ailments near the braziers that the road menders boiled their tar in, to benefit from the fumes that they gave off.

Because Ken Snr was to suffer continuous chest related illnesses such as, bronchitis and pneumonia, it was said that he was brought up on Angier's Emulsion. Its efficacy was not too well known and is described here,

"Angier's Emulsion was manufactured by the Angier Chemical Company beginning in the late 1800s and was sold world-wide throughout the mid 20th century. Angier's Emulsion

was originally compounded and marketed as a "food-medicine" and cure for a variety of respiratory ailments. The principle ingredient of this product was refined petroleum oil. Studies carried out as early as 1884 demonstrated that petroleum oil has no nutritional value. In response, Angier Chemical Company reformulated the product and marketed it as a laxative for "temporary constipation relief." However, the notion that Angier's Emulsion helped sooth membranes, including those of the respiratory tract continued to be prominently featured in advertisements, which promoted this product's use to treat influenza infection and other respiratory illnesses."

In those days it was common to see tiny coffins leaving the streets on their way to the cemetery, as well as mothers who had died in childbirth.

Ken's Mum, Clara, was often in demand as the midwife's helper. The expectant Mum would often send for her before the mid-wife arrived. Their gratitude for this help was only too apparent when Clara died. There were many small posies from the children of the street, who she had helped to deliver, on her coffin.

There may have been gratitude from within the community but this can be contrasted with the fact that when Ken Snr was born in the workhouse hospital, his Dad Jack, after long days at work as a sawyer, had to go and chop wood at the hospital as payment for the care of his wife and baby.

A bit of research by my daughter, Jenny, who is just retiring from her job as a nurse in the NHS and with the help of Michael Pearson, who as part of his role with the NHS is archiving local historical NHS information at the Hull History centre, has revealed the following article about the former Workhouse where my husband was born.

"Remembering the vital role played by Hull's infirmary during World War One.

The new 220-bed infirmary, then part of the Hull Workhouse, was handed over to the British Government to receive injured military personnel from the frontline after war was declared within days of its official opening.

To mark the centenary of the end of World War One, Hull and

LIFE IS WHAT YOU MAKE IT

East Yorkshire Hospitals NHS Trust is releasing photographs of a royal visit by King George and Queen Mary in 1917.

Hospital archivist Mike Pearson said: "The hospital played an important role in the history of the nation, long before the creation of the NHS. Trainloads of wounded soldiers and sailors were brought into the city and many of them owed their lives to the dedication and commitment of the staff who worked at the infirmary."

The infirmary, built on the current site of the current tower block, was opened by Hull Lord Mayor JH Hargreaves on July 16, 1914. However, Germany declared war on France and invaded neutral Belgium on August 3, with Britain declaring war on Germany the following day.

Hull handed over the infirmary to the War Office at York on August 15 with the Dowager Lady Nunburnholme offering to pay for the building to be equipped with stores and provisions.?It was to be used to treat casualties from the military and navy with the East Riding Territorial Branch of the St John Ambulance Association Voluntary Aid Committee supplying nurses and staff. The hospital started accepting casualties almost immediately and between August 1914 and January 1917, almost 2,500 patients, mainly soldiers and military personnel, were treated in Hull.

By January 31st, 1917, Britain's naval base hospitals were under intense pressure because of the number of casualties from the war at sea so the Admiralty asked that the hospital should only accept naval casualties. Six large and six smaller wards were used to treat 204 men and 16 officers. They were brought into the city on board Royal Naval ambulance trains as well as on scheduled services every Wednesday. A matron and twelve trained sisters ran the wards with the nurses coming from the Kingston and Western Division of the St John Ambulance Association Voluntary Aid Detachment.

King George and Queen Mary visited the hospital, speaking to staff and patients on June 18th,1917.

By the time the hospital closed in January 1919 following the end of the war, it had treated a further 4,000 patients."

Hull University Teaching Hospitals, NHS Trust

Thank goodness for the N.H.S.

King George and Queen Mary's visit to Hull on June 18th,1917.

LIFE IS WHAT YOU MAKE IT
SCHOOL

We now move to 1933 when Kenneth and I began our first days at school. I wet my pants and Kenneth cried a lot, two children finding it rather daunting. The buildings themselves with huge staircases and doors, windows that you could not reach, getting lost in a maze of corridors was too much for quite some time for us to accept.

The journey for me to get to school was across Hessle Road to Constable Street. It was then that I met the man who saw me across every day to school. I saw him as a friend, the jolly policeman, no doubt he helped me to settle down with always a friendly word. All of the kids loved him. His name was Bobby Harrison.

Kenneth unfortunately missed out on much of his early schooling because of ill health. His school was Daltry Street, with no main road to cross. The one thing that was keeping him going now that he was six years old was the school kids street outing.

The grown ups put in 2p each week for 12 months to pay for this outing to the seaside. For many of these children it was the only visit that they could expect until the next year. This was Kenneth's first. As it got nearer for the time for the vehicles to arrive, the air became electric. The Mum's all busy making sandwiches, mainly of potted meat or jam. All the kids in new sandshoes and clean shirts, bought on tick, all gathering at each terrace end.

Then the first coach came around the corner. The word went round and the cheering and laughing began. Imagine a line of vehicles right down the street, the kids dancing and shrieking, the adults trying to control the youngsters and at the same time boxes and bags of bottles of tap water were going on board.

Then came the order, "All aboard."

Young Ken thought that he was in heaven, this was his first trip. All of the Mums shouting, "Behave yourselves or you won't go next year!"

The time came for the magic moment to move out.

Kenneth was rather a quiet lad; always content to be a spectator looking on and enjoying the other lad's antics but the one thing that he was good at was singing. And sing they did all the way to Withernsea.

Schools and education have always been important to our family and a decent education has been one way for different generations to move on in their lives and perhaps improve their living conditions. It was one of the main reasons for me and Ken Snr, deciding to move off Hessle Road, before the demolition in the 1980's, to try to give our children the best chances possible through better schools. Not that my eldest son, who was more than happy at West Dock Avenue and Francis Askew, would agree, as he suffered through the stigma of being, 'off Hessle Road'.

It is interesting to note however that all of my sons, in one way or another have worked in schools during their adult lives.

Perhaps we did make the right move and for the right reasons.

ST ANDREWS DOCK

Central to most of the lives of the people written about in this book and to their way of life in many different ways, is St Andrews Dock or Fish Dock as it more commonly known in Hull. It was originally earmarked for use as a coal dock but by the time it was finished and officially opened on 24th September 1883, it was full of fishing boats. The dock got it's name from the patron saint of fishermen.

As well as the trawlermen who came and went with each tide, the dock employed people in many different jobs. Almost all of these involved dangerous work, particularly trawling, and Health and Safety was unheard of. Over the decades there have been many deaths and serious, life changing injuries, within the fishing industry and things came to a head in the winter of 1968 when 3 trawlers went down, over a period of a few days, in terrible conditions off Iceland. All but one of the crews were lost and a woman called Lily Bilocca had had enough and began a protest against the trawler owners to improve safety conditions on board trawlers. Accompanied by Yvonne Blenkinsop and Mary Denness and a union convener named John Prescott, they led a campaign, which was covered by the national media and managed to travel to Parliament and get the laws changed.

When the trawlers arrived from the fishing grounds in the Arctic, off Norway, Iceland and Russia, with some fishing as far as the banks off Newfoundland, their catches had to be unloaded.

This was the work of the Bobbers, who got their curious name from dodging the baskets of fish brought up from the hold by the Winchman and swung out onto the dockside where the Bobbers would catch them and tip the fish into kits, weighing out 10 stones each.

Waiting barrowlads would move the kits into their positions on the fish market and a dutch auction would take place. A dutch auction is when a top starting price was given and the fish merchants, atop the rows of kits would wait for the price to come down in stages, before bidding. It was a case of who could hold their nerve the longest to get the best price.

When the fish merchants bought their fish, they proceeded to lay 'tallies' on their kits, which were pieces of paper about the size of a bank note, with the fish merchant's name printed on it. The tallies came in all sorts of colours and they were much prized by the children of the fish dock workers, who used them as pretend money, tickets and whatever their imaginations could drum up.

The bought fish was then barrowed to the merchants premises which stood at the back of the quay, with an office above and a 'cave" underneath. The cave was a cold storage area used for the fish that wasn't sold or waiting to be collected. In front of the cave were the filleting benches, where the fish were filleted and packed into fish boxes.

At the back of the quay was a cobbled area where originally horses and rullies would collect and distribute the fish. Later it was trucks and trains that took the fish to the local fishmongers, smoke houses, fish shops and out across the country but probably the most important means of transport were on the fish dockworkers feet. Everyone wore clogs. They protected the feet but also stopped then slipping and in really wet and icy conditions they would look like they were skating as they moved around the quayside.

To get a job on fish dock was prized, as it paid well and Ken started on the dock as a barrowlad but he became a Bobber and a skilled Filleter. Later in life he owned a Fish and Chip Shop with me and eventually he became a Fish Monger with a Fish Round, travelling all over Holderness selling wet fish to villagers

Ken Chatwin Snr, tipping the basket as a 'bobber'

and farmers, from his blue Bedford van.

As we have already heard, I was one of the office staff working for a Fish Merchant on the dock.

Other trades that kept locals in employment included, net braiders, ice house workers, cod farm workers who dried fish in the open on racks, ships chandlers, engineers who kept the fishing fleet working,

Smokehouse workers who made the famous kippers and smoked fish in the curiously shaped buildings, a few of which still survive along Hessle Road. My Dad, Jim was a kipper smoker.

St Andrews's Dock was fringed by rows and rows of terraced houses, which all ran up to Hessle Road. Most of the families in those houses would have made their living from the fish dock in one-way or another.

Over the decades, deep sea fishing became more and more efficient in catching fish, the trawlers changed from sail to coal and oil power. They got bigger and the traditional, Sidewinders which could go out fishing for about three weeks, were eventually replaced with bigger Stern fishers and eventually Freezers which were huge factory ships that could stay away in the fishing grounds for much longer periods.

Unfortunately, as Ken often predicted, the trawler owners became too greedy and when one of the main fishing grounds, in Icelandic waters was being out fished, Iceland threw up restriction zones leading to the infamous Cod Wars and the eventual demise of the, once great, fishing industry in Hull.

St Andrew's fish dock was eventually closed on 3rd November 1975, when the few remaining trawlers transferred into the Albert and William Wright Docks, where a massively reduced trade in fish is still plied, ironically much of the fish coming from Icelandic Trawlers.

Hessle Road began to run down and eventually the Hessle roaders were dispersed to large housing estates, away from the dock area.

ENTERTAINMENT

As I give some thought to entertainment and how it had changed over the decades, the adults had variety Theatres and Music Halls, Cinemas, Pubs, Football, Rugby League, Cricket amongst the ways that they would pass their time when not at work.

There wasn't much money for entertainment and so the youngsters had their street games including marbles, ciggy cards, peggy stick, ball games including football and cricket, block hoop racing, rope games including skipping, hopscotch and chalking pictures on the pavements.

Many of the games were 'made up', just for the fun of it and we would pool any coppers that we had to buy something special and then share it.

Despite the war years, things seemed to be safer in the years before and after the conflict and so with less traffic, it was more common for younger children to be allowed to play 'out on the streets' and even at quite young ages for us to wander further afield to such places as the Humber foreshore, Pickering Park and Little Switzerland. The latter was a series of abandoned chalk quarries with a very deep lake, which were a natural wonderland for kids to play in. There were occasional accidents and even tragedies but they were part of growing up.

When there was a bit of money to spare, then there were lots of cinemas and quite a few swimming baths.

STREET PARTIES

Bigger events were celebrated communally such as bonfire night, the end of war and Coronations, usually with street parties.

For example the abdication of the Prince of Wales, was such a shock to the public but the following coronation of his brother was another excuse for a 'street party'.

My Grandma made me a white dress with red and blue trimmings as I had been invited to the next street, Walcott Street, where they had pianos outside in the terraces, which was made possible by coverings of tarpaulins. It seems like any excuse was used for these events where furniture was brought out of the houses and everyone would contribute something, no matter how poor and small.

A SUNDAY TREAT

I and the boys, while still small, if the weather allowed, were taken walking to the Pier and Horse wash, known locally as 'Osswash'. Many other families enjoyed the same pastime.

This was in the town, situated between the River Hull and

LIFE IS WHAT YOU MAKE IT

Princess Dock, on the banks of the Humber Estuary, where they would mingle with the crowds watching the Humber Ferry approaching the pier at our side of the river, after crossing from a place called New Holland, in Lincolnshire.

The pier was a double decked, wooden promenade structure and a favourite leisure place for lots of families.

The carriers would bring their big dray horses down a cobbled slope into the water where they scrubbed them clean. A treat for the horses as well, as they were housed in stables when not working.

The kids revelled in so much space, poking things through the planking to see it being washed away by the river and sometimes they would have ice cream before home time.

CINEMAS

The cinema became most of the youngsters number one entertainment, all waiting for the Saturday Matinee to come around each week and for the grand sum of 2d and ?d for toffee, they were entertained by their heroes – Flash Gordon, Buck Jones, Tom Mix, Roy Rodgers, Hop-a-long Cassidy and after the show they would gallop home to re-enact to their hearts content.

From the moment that he saw his first film, Ken Snr became obsessed, mainly with Westerns, to the point that in later teenage years, his earnings as a paperboy were spent almost entirely in the many Cinemas that could be found along Hessle Road and neighbouring streets and roads. The 'Queen' of cinemas on Hessle Road was Langham. It had a beautiful foyer with a wide staircase that opened up as it ascended to the balcony or 'the Gods' as it was often known. After the hardship and horrors of the war and the poverty that followed, cinema was a place for escapism and the grand entrance to cinemas like Langham was the start of the journey into a fantasy world of films, excitement and glamour.

Probably the opposite to the grandeur of the Langham was the Eureka Cinema, also known as 'Laugh and Scratch" as it had a reputation for not being too clean. At he other end of Hessle Road in Gypsyville you could walk to the Regis and only a short bus ride or walk into town were the Tower and Regent, Dorchester, Criterion also known as the Cri, the ABC and the sumptuous Cecil.

I also had a very early cinematic experience, as my Mam told me that she was present at one of the first screenings of the first full length feature film with speech in some parts, "The Jazz Singer", starring Al Jolson, not that she could remember anything about it as she was a baby in her mother's arms

Ken Senior's love of the cinema was passed down to Ken Jnr, who in fact was often his father's excuse to spend his afternoons (he worked night's on the Fish Dock) on the prairies of the Wild West or fighting the Germans and Japanese in the war, which had only ended a few years before.

To this day Ken Jnr can still remember the films that he saw with his Dad or sometimes his Mam and Nanny and they included; Davey Crockett, Shane, Calamity Jane, Seven Brides For Seven Brothers, The River of No Return and Old Yellow. John Wayne, Gary Cooper, Sophia Loren, Robert Ryan and Robert Mitchum were amongst the many filmstars that they saw on a regular basis but Ken Jnr remembers that his Dad's real love were the 'B' movies which were usually, black and white, American Crime thrillers now known as Film Noir, which it appears could only be fully appreciated by 'grown ups' as Ken Jnr had to tolerate them before getting to the 'big film'. To keep his attention, Ken Jnr was usually told by his Dad that the big film had, 'a big fight at the end'. This was not always true.

SWIMMING BATHS

Another favourite pastime was swimming. The swimming and washing or slipper baths as they were known, on Hessle Road were down Madeley Street.

They were built in 1885 and provided a place to get a hot bath and swim, as non of the houses down Hessle Road and it's many terraces, would have had hot water or bathrooms but to the children they were a popular place to have some fun. With individual changing cubicles around the side of the baths, rows of benches for spectators and a balcony they were a regular haunt for many Hessle Road kids. Even though there was a quite high diving board many would show off by jumping from the balcony, at the risk of being thrown out. Ken Snr gained his swimming certificates from school at Madeley Street baths. Other uses for this public facility were that people could get a hot bath and in the winter, on Saturdays the pool was transformed into a Dance

Hall, with a wooden floor covering the pool. This is where Ken and I first met. Madeley Street was also a popular venue for wrestling.

CELEBRATIONS

Christmas, New Year, Easter, Holidays, Hull Fair and Bonfire Night, have all been celebrated by the families throughout the generations and across this book with some changing in a number of ways but all became milestone or stepping stones which break up the often tedious grind of working people.

CHRISTMAS AND NEW YEAR

Sadly, money and media have all played a part in making all of these celebrations somehow less festive and the old stories of an orange, an apple, a sixpence and maybe a small toy for Christmas might be a little exaggerated with time but the one thing that seems to have persisted across the decades is that all of these annual events were a good excuse for a family get together. Even fishing boats would try to be back in the dock for Christmas. Not all made it and the ones that did had quite a job to get a crew to go back out before New Year.

In the lead up to Christmas, children would earn extra pocket money from the 'tips' that were given by customers on their Saturday jobs, 'paper rounds' and from carol singing.

It was also traditional at the times of these main celebrations that many would get new clothes. These were often made by their mothers or bought with 'club cards' from shops such as Clothing House and part of the festive routine would be when families 'promenaded' their new attire.

The large houses 'down Boulevard' would display huge Christmas trees in their bay windows, beautifully decorated with tinsel and baubles, with smaller ones down the terraces.

The shops of Hessle Road would be festooned with Christmas trimmings and the white-wash signs, handwritten on the windows describing the Christmas delights that they were selling, particularly the butchers where, depending on finances, families would buy their Christmas meats and pork pies. Grocers for the vegetables and of course the toyshops for toys and other gifts. Many ran a Christmas Club where people could save throughout the year to make sure that they could afford something come Christmas.

Once the shops finally closed for Christmas and they all did, the streets would become unusually quiet until the revelry began on Christmas Eve when the pubs, clubs and people's houses became alive with people celebrating, not only Christmas but also one of the few opportunities to let their hair down, as most people would not have to be up for work the next day.

Everyone will have their own memories of their family Christmases and most would be happy, centred around waking to presents and a Christmas dinner, prepared almost entirely by the womenfolk in the families, while the men went out for a few drinks and to swap stories about the goings on of the night before. These would often include talk of when the alcohol got the better of some of the revellers and as well as the singing and laughter, fights would spill out of pubs, clubs and houses onto the streets. The following day with black eyes and thick heads, the sheepish participants would try to remember how they got their battle scars and drink again with those who they had been fighting with.

For the children, the times around the Christmas dinner would be for parading their Christmas presents on the unusually quiet streets. Girls would be pushing dollies in their new prams or with the boys riding their new bikes often dressed in cowboy or indian costumes. For most it was an opportunity to drink and eat more than usual and New Year's Eve was another great excuse for a celebration and the women, as on Christmas Eve, had to book very early to get their 'hair done' for the coming night out. People would make their way, early, to their favourite pub or club, of which there were many down Hessle Road, to make sure of a table and these included Tim's and Dee Street Clubs that were small, almost 'speakeasy' style premises, bigger establishments such as The Phoenix and the many pubs including Rayners the fishermen's pub, Criterion and Half-way House also filled up for Christmas and New Year's Eve celebrations.

New Year celebrations followed much the same pattern as Christmas, the week before and come New Years day there would be a repeat of the heavy heads and stories from the night before.

LIFE IS WHAT YOU MAKE IT

EASTER

As with Christmas, Easter was a predominant religious festival, which was to a large extent highjacked as a time for families to celebrate local customs. The religious part of these festivals was most often observed and celebrated through schools but within families, Easter was celebrated through treats such as decorated hard boiled eggs and chocolate eggs and family events such as days out or trips to the local parks and maybe even cinemas. For the adults it would again be a short break from their daily working lives.

SUMMER HOLIDAYS

Holidays were only just beginning to become possible for working people around the middle of the 1800's and these were usually 'Holy days', which is where we get the word Holiday from. These would be on religious festivals and as Jane Forth grew up, various laws were introduced to ensure paid holidays on top of the days such as New Year's Day which became known as Bank Holidays but for most working people living around Hessle Road a day out might be the only holiday that was affordable. Trains began to provide cheaper forms of transport to places further away from Hessle Road than the local parks and the 'seaside resorts' such as Withernsea, Hornsea, Bridlington, Filey Scarborough and Whitby began to appear as destinations for those who could afford longer holidays.

The further up the East Coast that families took their holidays, in caravans and boarding houses, was often an indication as to how well the fishing industry was doing. When there had been a bad year maybe there would be no holiday at all, a better year might see a trip for our families to Skipsea or Withernsea but a good year might mean a week in Bridlington or even Scarborough.

There is only any evidence or mention of holidays after Jane Forth's lifetime with Jinnie and Jim and Ken and I and family travelling to one of the East Coast holiday villages and eventually by the 1960s a stay at Butlins Holiday Camp caused a great deal of excitement. Later in the book we can read about our families travel to more exotic holiday destinations.

HULL FAIR

After the summer holidays came to an end children's thoughts began to turn to the annual visit of Hull Fair and how they could earn and save pocket money for this weeklong event.

Locals have always boasted that Hull Fair is the biggest travelling fair in Europe and there is evidence to prove this to be true.

One thing for certain is that the fair dates back centuries to as early as the 1200s and it has been so popular that there was once a riot on the streets of Hull when it was threatened that a calendar change in the 1700's was going to end the fair. It is often said that it also marked the end of the whaling season in October but whether this is true or not the week in October has always been awaited by Hull families with a great deal of anticipation.

It has also certainly been a part of the festive year from Jane Forth's time across all of the generations in this book.

Some of the earlier generations would have been attracted into the 'freak shows' of human giants, bearded ladies, deformed animals and performing flea circuses. Boxing booths and other physical challenges such as punch bags and 'ring the bell with a sledge hammer' were also part of many sideshows that lined the streets.

The rides at the fair have become more and more spectacular and food has always played a part in the experience, with brandy snap, candy floss, toffee apples, roast chestnuts and Bob Carvers stall where you could buy Hull's famous Pattie and Chips amongst other chip shop food.

In the past some of these foods only appeared in Hull around Hull Fair, such as the exotic pomegranates.

At the end of a night's excitement on the rides, enough money would be saved for the purchase of a toy from the many stalls and favourites within our family have been plastic swords and guns, cowboy and indian outfits and fairy dolls with their different coloured net costumes.

BONFIRE NIGHT

Next on the calendar of annual celebrations was Guy Fawkes Night. Gangs of kids from the different streets would begin collecting wood and scrap for their bonfires and raids would be made on neighbouring streets piles.

Also as part of the lead up to the big night on 5th November you could find on many street corners, kids asking passers by for a 'penny for the guy' as they displayed their home made figures dressed in old clothes and usually sitting in an old tansad or pram. Sometimes the figures turned out not to be scarecrows but badly made up children sitting very still.

Ken Chatwin told stories of the individual streets on Hessle Road building their bonfires in the middle of the roads, sometimes more than one in a street and of the disappointment of the residents when the Fire Brigade turned out to put the fires out!

THE FISH ROUND

As Jenny reached four years old and Ken talking about a fish round for sale and leaving work as a bobber, he made an offer and became a fishmonger.

My parents offered to have young Jenny until Ken became used to this new venture, with me to assist him for a few months. Of course it was like a duck to water for Ken. He enjoyed being out in the countryside and his customers were friendly people, so friendly on these rounds that he was soon like their friendly postman, delivering Mrs Smith's daughter's washing in the next village or letting the farmers wife know that the pigs are in her vegetable patch! One day I remember that we were in between villages when I spotted one of the farmers wives in the distance running like mad on the road and as we got closer we could see why. There was a young pig enjoying its freedom. We both decided to help her take hold of it, then realized that she had to get back to the farm and so we ended up with the farmers wife, with a pig on her knee in the front seat of the van. This was just one of many stories that we were part of during the next seven years.

After the first few months, Ken decided that he only needed me to help for two days a week and I had to admit that it had been tiring me, rising early and trying to run the house, washing for six, plus all of the white fish coats needed for work on the round. It also relieved Mum of caring for Jenny who was now three years old. The boys were getting older and able to earn their pocket money by doing the washing up etc.

THE BOAT

After brother Bill had left the sea, he became a pub landlord, which was quite common for trawler skippers, and one of the pubs that he ran was across the river at a place called South Ferriby, where the River Ancholme joins the Humber Estuary.

On one of our visits on the old ferry across the Humber, (this was before the Humber Bridge was built), Ken overheard a conversation about a boat for sale at the other side. My brother Bill already owned one and the next thing that I knew, Ken had put in a bid. On the way home he told me, "Don't worry Joyce, the bid is far too low to be accepted."

We were soon to discover that we now owned a boat, which had never been in the water!! Indeed it was a snip.

Much fun was had by all of the family.

One experience was the day that we sailed through crowds of people waving at us from the banks of the river. Naturally we waved back then when we turned a bend in the river it began to dawn on us that we were in the middle of a regatta. There was bunting and flags and a Commodore in uniform, who was not at all pleased with our arrival, especially as our three little Yorkshire Terriers made themselves known from their position on the stern.

The sun was shining, everyone with flags and blowing horns. We thoroughly enjoyed ourselves and so did the dogs.

A less enjoyable experience on the boat was an incident that involved our son Bill. While using the tiny toilet facility on one trip, an over enthusiastic river user, in a large speedboat sped by and created a huge wash, which in turn rocked the boat so violently that it threw Bill off the toilet and caused him to bang his head on the door, which in turn threw it open and ejected him from the toilet compartment into the main cabin area. I'm not sure what hurt him the most, his head or the humiliation but it gave the rest of us a great laugh and another story for posterity.

The River Ancholme is only navigable for about 20 miles, into the Lincolnshire countryside, but we had some great times pottering up and down it's length, stopping in the villages and towns such as Brigg, fishing and even swimming on the warmer summer days.

THE PONY

I should point out that our family were fairly average folk but every now and again something turns up out of the blue. One such occasion was when Jenny answered the doorbell to some girls who were running a raffle for a pony no less. Jenny had in fact become interested in riding just recently. The raffle was two shillings and sixpence (half a crown), which big brother Ken Jnr promptly gave her, saying that we never win anything Mam. Having said this, a few days later a telephone message informs me that we had won a pony!

The pony in question was unbroken and we quickly converted, part of the back of the garage into a stable, with a stable door!

Breaking the pony in was quite a spectacle for us and the neighbours, as someone practiced in this art carried out the training in our back garden.

Eventually proper stabling was found out near Ferriby and after a time it had to be admitted that it was just a bit too much for us to manage and so it was sold to a good home.

THE ISLE OF SKYE

The year 1981 turned out to be a pretty eventful one for the family. We were six in number, two parents and four adult offspring; three sons and a daughter, just beginning nurse training. Son no. 1, Ken, photographer for Hull City Council. Son no.2, Bill, who is by this time teaching and Son no.3, Mark, working as a mechanic.

Bad news begins to break with Ken senior's redundancy, closely followed by Ken Jnr. It soon became clear that this was cutback time for employees and then it was Mark to lose his job. A traumatic and frightening period for the people who were to lose their jobs. It appears that the politicians still can't do their sums right.

The family began to make plans for their future, rather hurriedly and Ken Snr was utterly demoralized and became so unhappy that I decided to go along with any plan that he may have in mind. The plan, as it turned out, was to move to Scotland.

The feeling of wanting to escape from the rat race seemed to run through the family but leaving her (my) daughter behind in Leeds where she had started her nurse training was tearing her (me) to pieces. Also Bill and Chrissie now with a baby girl, Melody. This was one of the most unhappy times in her (my) life. No, this was not going to be easy – not at all.

She (Mam) had to come to terms with the inevitable and the

only way she could do this was by telling herself to find a loophole if things did not work out in other words, a back door.

The decision was made.

The house was sold and so at the beginning of October 1981, Ken and the boys going on before myself, saw me leaving leaving Bill on the platform at Leeds railway station to see me safely aboard the train.

The destination was the Isle of Skye and the whole train journey consisted of a stop off to change at Edinburgh. The next change at Inverness and then on to the Kyle of Lochalsh.

I can never forget the tears I shed all the way from Leeds to Newcastle that day. I couldn't forget my daughter's eyes following me as I left the bedroom and later in life I was to put myself back to memories of my own mother in 1939, when I was leaving to be evacuated and thought, "this was how she must have felt".

When I eventually arrived in the evening at Kyle of Lochalsh, I remember that Ken was there to meet me then we boarded the Island Ferry to go on our way to the village towards the top part of the island, called Edinbane, which sits on the shores of a sea loch called Loch Greishornish.

By this time I was very tired and was very surprised when Ken insisted that he took me into the local hotel to meet our next-door neighbour, who's name was 'Spider'. He was also a regular entertainer at The Edinbane Hotel and all that I wanted was a good night's sleep.

A croft is, strictly speaking, a piece of land which usually has a cottage or other dwelling built on it but in Scotland it is usually the term used for the cottage built on the land.

Our croft (cottage) consisted of a kitchen, living room, two bedrooms running out off a passage, a bathroom and one tiny room off the living room. Our address was Upper Edinbane, it being up a hill. Our energy in the cottage was electric and coal, plus wood and the traditional peat.

Naturally there were many differences between Yorkshire born city dwellers and the local folk.

We learned for ourselves how troublesome certain things, such as Social Administration can be – slowly – slowly – slowly or never!

Naturally we realised this was not going to be a picnic. No work and we had to survive, carefully adapting to the needs of 4 people. We held meetings to discuss how, what and where would we manage financially.

It was to be that after six months of waiting we decided to face up to the authorities. To do this we had to make the journey from Skye across to Inverness, where a signed missing form had already been in the office for four months. Ken received his six months allowances, due to him, immediately.

The cottage was being rented to us until it was released from the croft. We certainly did not think that it still hadn't been passed by the courts in Edinburgh until we discovered that the person or daughter of the owner called 'Maggie Anne', now deceased, was not the person that the cottage had been left to, hence the delay.

In the meantime we were accepted by our neighbours. Ken went with Spider to help with the sheep count and dipping. Mark was fixing cars until he found work at Broadford in a boat yard. Ken Snr joined up with Uisjon, Spiders brother, selling fish that the small fishing boats had landed at Dunvegan harbour, around the island. Then the news went around that they needed men on the mainland where they were building an oil-rig at Kishorne. Ken Jnr signed on.

Now going back to December 1981, I had been having sleepless nights over Jenny. Ken was also unsettled about this. Before we left for Skye, we had promised Jenny and my parents that we would come back to visit at Christmas. The whole of Britain was white with snow and ice. We couldn't have chosen a worse time to make such a journey. The journey was pretty scary but we witnessed scenes the like of which we had never seen before. Picture snow scenes on picture postcards – hills and mountains with cottages tucked away in valleys and everything white and as we began to turn the car south, light turned to dusk and we didn't see another car on the road for mile after mile. The snow was lighting everything up and then the moon came out from behind the clouds in time for us to witness a very large herd of deer that had all come down from the hills, with the stag standing up on a large rock keeping guard. They were

The croft (cottage) at
Upper Edinbane, above
Loch Cgrshornish, Isle of Skye

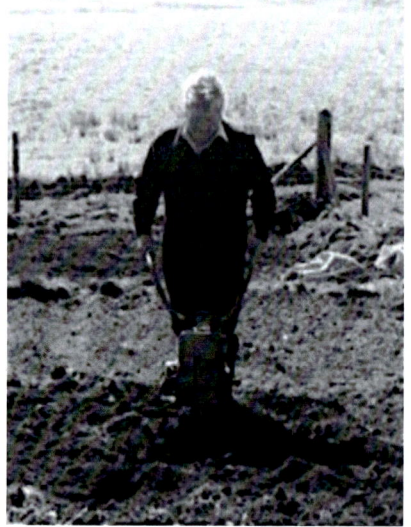

**Ken creating our new
garden with his new rotivator**

everywhere, this is where we practically had to come to a standstill to avoid hitting them. It was sheer magic, the silence both inside the car and outside was eerie, the noise from these beautiful animals was just the odd snorting they make from ourselves the odd ooh and ahh and so we left them behind having driven through this very large herd, very slow indeed, without one casualty. Ken reckoned there was well over a hundred.

We eventually made it south to Leeds to pick up Jenny after being diverted many, many times due to the extreme weather conditions. We passed dozens of trucks abandoned along the motorways. Ken was heard to mention the fact, 'lucky we brought the metal wheel tracks."

After a welcome re-union with Jenny we then made for my parents house to stay over Christmas. After keeping our promise to my parents things began to feel as though this visit was turning a little sad.

One week later we attempted a return journey. For one thing Ken and myself found ourselves not wanting to leave Jenny behind again. Ken began to voice his opinions stating that he would not leave without her and so began plans to meet with the NHS authorities for Jenny to be freed from her contract. This was agreed and so off we went once again up the motorway back to Skye. That return journey was softened for me with the fact that I had my daughter with me once again and I don't think I would have been so willing had she not been.

When we returned to the ferry crossing in the early hours of the morning all very tired after freezing conditions, bad snow storms and the like, we were all so surprised to feel something very different. The men got out of the car and smiled at each other turning to us they reported it was warm, no wind, no snow, just very calm and warm.

It was unbelievable. It does prove that the Gulf Stream does work! Especially after what we had experienced.

So Jenny said, 'Hello,' to the neighbours and became welcomed as another one of the Chatwin clan.

The cottage was now beginning to look much improved. Ken and the lads had painted all of the rooms, the curtains and carpets were down and a good fire in the grate. Soon we were adapting to live within the Edinbane social habits, one of which included leaving your doors unlocked. This was necessary within a small community when help was needed such as doctors, fire fighters etc, especially transporting children or elderly night or day. The fire station and doctor's surgery were miles away, so your car had to be at their disposal also. In the months ahead we were to witness many events, some comical and some not so.

After our visit home to Hessle and returning with Jenny to celebrate New Year we quickly settled down to make plans.

Our neighbours in the next-door croft, were Alister, known as Spider and Mary McSwann and their two children, a boy and a girl and just a few steps up the hill was Alister's mother's croft. She was known by all as Granny. Next up the hill lived Dan and Flora McNab with their two offspring and further up still were Dorothy and Ralph.

Just across the road from our croft lived Janet and James with two girls and on the road going downhill to the loch were many more crofts and the garage come shop where you collected your morning newspapers at teatime!

Ken and his two sons were soon part of village life, while Jenny and myself became cooks, cleaners and bottle washers most days!! We began making plans for a garden and ordered seeds, most of which I raised on the window ledges.

During the festive week following New Year, Spider gathered men to tackle a chimney fire at Janet's across the road, including Ken, who I told to bring the family to our croft, including a new baby. When the firemen arrived the fire was out and so they all had a drink as part of still celebrating New Year.

By now we had a coalman and dustmen and Ken and sons made regular trips to Portree, with the trailer to collect wood for our fire. Working life got into some kind of routine, which included Ken helping Spider with the sheep, Mark repairing the neighbours cars and Mark and Ken cockling on the shore of Loch Greshornish, in freezing cold conditions, selling them to lorries from Spain.

By April it was time to start preparing the garden, which I discovered was more like a rockery, so much so that I was making paths with the ruddy things. Ken, bless his cotton socks, was able to get me some manure from the postman's stables for my tatties, which were now sprouting. He also got a rotivator, to turn the previously uncultivated soil and the weather was improving. The garden was set on the side of a hill, so when it came to planting I had no option but kneeling or falling backwards. The bottom bit was level so Ken planted the tatties there. I now had a tray of leeks ready to plant. After planting a few, I noticed something moving them side to side and then they were disappearing. I was to discover that we had moles no less!

By June the weather really was improving and Ken at last had word from Dan McNab that he had found him a bog, meaning that we could begin to cut peats. The bog was about a mile away from the village and we were told that no one had worked the peats for quite a few years. The youngsters back at the village soon heard what we were up to and so we had them for company. One day a bus turned up, full of tourists, taking photos and I have to admit it is very hard work.

Two or three weeks later, Dan told us that the peats were dry enough to be moved back to the croft. That day, Dan's son, Donald came with a tractor and trailer to take the peats back to the village and who but all of the youngsters as well arrived with him.

While all of this was going on Ken Snr managed to sprain his ankle. Dan then had to drive our car, bringing me a drink, with all of the tourists watching this little woman in overalls cutting peats. He then drove us back to the croft, insisting that we stop on the way for a pint.

July turned into a really hot one and those who were on council water, like ourselves, had to ration water, with a stop to bathing everyday so that it could be saved for cooking and washing, some of the wives were even using the stream!

In the meantime it had been arranged for our son Bill's school pupils back in Leeds, to make their weeks holiday in Edinbane.

Ken Snr arranged for the caravans to let, down by the loch, for the accommodation for the teachers and pupils.

In the meantime, the next event to take place at Willy Shankey's, Edinbane Hotel, was a surprise. Everyone was instructed to wear Kilt's etc, as a German film crew wanted to film as authentic as possible, a Scottish ceilidh with music, monologues, poetry etc. There we all were, an audience, some English with borrowed kilts and a lovely fire burning in the

Me and Ken digging the peats
for our winter fuel

fireplace. A cameraman gave an order and Dan began to recite his monologue, then another order to, 'go back, go back' until someone shouted, 'If he goes any further back you'll have his arse on fire'.

With July on the way, we were making preparations to receive our teacher son Bill with his Headmaster, David Dewhirst, staff member Celia Foot and pupils. I began to realize that after a very long journey from Leeds, they would need refreshments and so we began making plans for meals to be ready on late arrival and early departure at the croft. We were already familiar with Bill's class and Headmaster as we were used to entertaining them when they made visits to our home back in East Yorkshire.

The day arrived when the school bus came up the hill and out poured the children, the teachers trying to keep order. One of the pupils broke away from the rest and he came flying down the hill towards me. I was waiting for them at the gate and the next minute he threw his arms around me and that was the beginning of settling them down. Mary, our neighbour helping Ken and myself with our visitors who thoroughly enjoyed their Scottish holiday.

Willy Shankey and Spider McSwann entertained them in true, traditional Scottish style in the Hotel. Mary's brother Uisdon (pronounced Ooshden) also gave a hand with his boat taking them out to see the seals and do a bit of fishing, off Dunvegan, where there is also Dunvegan Castle, which is the ancestral home of the Clan Macleod, which contains the famous Fairy Flag.

Another experience was made possible for them by Ken Jnr, who arranged for them to visit Kishorne, where he was working on the construction of an oil rig back on the mainland.

The day before their departure we were all invited out by David, the Head, to a meal as a thank you for our efforts with help and support, which we also enjoyed doing.

We had a meal in the village, fit for a king. Lobsters, crabs, clams and steaks, all presented beautifully at the local Inn.

The day of departure arrived. Breakfast had to be very early before they left, taking Jenny with them back to Yorkshire, as it had been arranged for her to escort her Grandparents, by train back to Skye for a holiday. After seeing the bus, with son Bill driving and daughter Jenny a passenger with the school party, disappearing down the hill, Ken turned to me and said, "I think that went well" and I had to agree that we were helped by our newly found friends in the village, both turning to go back in the cottage for a clear up and a cup of rosy lee. In the meantime we had to make preparations for my parents and Jenny who would be arriving the following week but little did we know what complications were about to develop.

The day for their arrival came and I began to prepare a lovely prawn salad with extra trimmings, which would be put in the fridge. That salad never reached the fridge. Never in a month of Sundays could we have been prepared for the message we were about to receive. I heard the phone ring and went to answer it. Jenny at the other end said, "Mam we are at Edinburgh station waiting for the next train to Inverness, (then a pause) but we have lost Granddad." With that message my heart sank. I shouted for Ken telling him, "My father's lost".

He took the phone from me straight away, then giving orders to Jenny of what she had to do and what he and myself were about to do, giving us all peace of mind. If anyone could sort it out, it was Ken bless him. Putting the phone down he turned to me saying that we were going to meet them in Inverness. Straight away the salad was packed into bread cakes with flasks of hot drinks and even cakes! In no time we were on the road to the ferry taking us to the mainland over to the Kyle of Lochalsh where we continued overland to Inverness.

After Ken got things sorted at the railway office, I was waiting to see any train bringing passengers in, when who should appear but my father. With Ken still in the office I took Dad to the car where the food and drink were. Naturally he wanted to see mother and Jenny who had not yet appeared! Then sitting with Dad he began to tell me what had happened.

Apparently arriving in York station, my father, not having travelled on trains since they were steam engines, told Jenny, "I want you to see to your Nanny, while I see to the luggage". Both of them did as he asked and got comfortable with the tickets and the packed lunch and they thought that Dad must have boarded the train further down. Then the whistle blew and off they began to move. After a while Jenny began asking one of the staff on the train and she began to look much further down but no sign of

Granddad. We discovered later that Dad, with the luggage, went looking for the Guards Van, which of course didn't exist anymore and the train eventually pulled out leaving him and the luggage on the platform. He then told the station staff what had happened and that his destination was Aberdeen, which was where he finally arrived from!

Meanwhile the train from Edinburgh was about to arrive and so Dad was left in the car while I waited for Mam and Jenny. Ken appeared telling me that; "they have put him on a train to us at Inverness". I then gave him a surprise, telling him to go to the car and stay and don't let him get away. Then of course we burst out laughing with relief. Mam and Jenny were not long appearing, Mam calling to me, "Have you found him".

After helping themselves to the salad tea we had to make a quick departure, for the long journey back to Kyle of Lochalsh, in order to catch the last ferry back onto the island.

This was not to be and we arrived too late and my parents went to a B&B for the night while we settled down in the car, near the loch, very tired.

All went well for the rest of their stay as we took them sightseeing. While they were with us Mark had been asked by a neighbour to take his boat out to lift his lobster pots. Mark, who was used to being out on boats and was a member of the Coastguard, took Jenny with him. Apparently they got the boat out, with everything going as normal until one of the ropes got caught on the propeller and they were drifting towards the rocks. Mark, stripped to his underpants, went overboard and dived repeatedly, under the boat, eventually cutting the propeller free. The waters up there are freezing cold and apart from cutting his back badly on the barnacles on the underneath of the boat, he got the job done. He was adventurous from birth.

We continued taking Mam and Dad around the places of interest, back to the mainland to Plockton, then to the famous Eileen Donan Castle, sitting out on Loch Duich, adding to their Scottish castle experiences with Dunvegan, the seat of Clan Macleod being another.

Eventually the time arrived for us to part company, when we heard on the television of a train strike.

Once more unto the breech... the comings and goings of my

parents on Skye left us all making fun and having a good laugh. And so once again, Ken started up the car and leaving Jenny in charge, we once more set off for Yorkshire.

When we arrived back at the croft my worries were even stronger concerning the fact that our eventual ownership of the croft had become doubtful, due to a loophole in Scottish law.

We discovered that the land laws were different to those back in England and while the land that the 'cottage' stood on was the croft, the land and the cottage were separate in law. As is common in those parts the whole parcel is known as 'the croft' and this is how I have referred to it throughout much of this account.

I began wrestling with should we stay or should we go and I eventually became anxious and depressed. Ken took the matter in hand. The next thing that I knew was that Ken wanted me to go back home and look for a house as he had closed the deal with the croft.

Leaving Ken and Jenny on the island, it was another early start a few days later when they put me on the train. It had made things so much easier, having had the phone installed, thus being able to make arrangements with Mam and Dad back home, where I was to stay.

Eventually things began to happen when we bought a small house with a small garden in Bristol Road, Hull. It was very run down but we soon put things right, when once we were together again.

Mark returned with his Dad and Jenny, to help move us back down and set up the house but returned to Scotland and his future wife, Caroline Macleod, to return permanently to Hull later. Meanwhile Ken Jnr stayed up at Applecross, working on the oil rigs and he would eventually return to England a few years later with his future wife, Wendy Mayfield but to Quorn near Nottingham and not to Hull.

Bill and Christina were well established in Leeds with their first-born, Melody.

When Mark did eventually return permanently to Hull, he and his Dad found work as dustmen for a short spell and I became an office cleaner for the N.H.S.

Gradually we settled back at home, with everyone back in

work and Jenny returning to her nurse training but we will always remember our adventure on Skye. We often have holidays back up in Scotland.

FAMILY EVENTS

Time moved on with all of the normalities of family life, including weddings, births and health problems. Some of the key family events I will record here, briefly, perhaps not chronologically but most importantly to imprint them within this family history.

Sarah Hodgson

The year was 1990 when on the morning of January 1st, my brother Jim opened the front door to find a police officer standing there to give Jim and Janet, the sad news that Sarah, their youngest daughter of 17 years of age, had died in an accident during a visit to her boyfriend in Holland.

She was a beautiful young girl, full of fun and loved by everyone. The level of shock and grief that Jim and Janet felt at that moment, we will never know.

Tracey Hodgson

The following year, 1991, on January 2nd my brother Jim's family were to face a second tragic loss of their eldest daughter Tracey, who had been rushed into hospital, very ill, never to recover. These times for Jim and Janet and their family, with their son Howard and daughter Kaye, must have been and still must be unimaginable.

David Hodgson

My other brother Bill and his wife Betty, were to have their own tragic family loss on 3rd July 2011.

They had two sons. Paul who had joined the forces and David who as well as other ventures such as bar owner, became a ship's Bursar on cruise ships travelling around the world. Unfortunately on one of these trips he became very ill and had to be put ashore and in July 2011 he passed away.

A loving young man who would dance all night in disco's around the world.

Ken Chatwin Jnr

As already mentioned Ken stayed up in Scotland for some time after we returned to Hull and there he met Wendy and they eventually returned to Quorn and then moved up to Leeds and had two sons, Jack and Brigham. Another move took them out to a cottage outside Keighley. Sadly their marriage ended and Ken moved, with his two sons back to the coast, where they now enjoy life in Hornsea.

Bill Chatwin

After studying in Leeds Bill became a teacher and met Christina (or Chrissie as she is known), who was also from East Yorkshire, Cottingham to be precise. They married, settled in Leeds and had their three children, Melody, Abigail and Liam.

Melody met Phil Nickson and they have two lovely children, Isabelle and Theo (my great grandchildren).

Abigail became a teacher and eventually moved to a teaching job in the Caribbean Island of Cayman, where she is still, as I write.

Liam became a music technician and DJ/Producer, started his own record label and now lives most of the year, with his Spanish partner Paula in southern Spain.

Mark Chatwin

Mark and Caroline moved down to Hull, where they married and began their family, having two boys James and Thomas.

James showed a particular skill with I.T. and Tom became a joiner. Sadly Mark and Caroline became divorced.

Jenny Chatwin

As with Mark, Jenny has played a significant part in the latter stages of my and Ken's lives. On her return from Skye, Jenny qualified as a nurse and has since worked at Hull and East Riding hospitals, mainly in Castle Hill Hospital. She has just begun her semi-retirement.

I was still putting my sewing machine to good use and enjoying my gardening working on my small piece of garden together with my own greenhouse. On one side were the tomatoes and opposite sat my potted flowers.

Ken Snr soon found permanent work in a factory nearby making baths and sinks. I have to add that he got the job by giving his age as ten years younger than he was! I returned to being a full time housewife.

ANOTHER HOUSE MOVE

As time moved forward, the older we became and the ailments increased as to be expected but we each looked after one another and we blessed each day for the NHS.

We eventually took the decision to put down our names for a council pensioners bungalow and sell the house. We were successful in our application and our new address became 20, Sandycroft Close, Willerby Road, Hull.

Ken's health, by this time was needing more of his doctor's attention and it was on one of our many visits to the surgery, in Marmaduke Street, Hessle Road that we were to witness the beginnings of the now infamous flooding in Hull.

THE FLOODS

The year is 2007 as Ken and myself boarded the bus to pay a visit to the doctor's. The rain was coming down in sheets by the time we reached the surgery in Marmaduke Street. We were both soaking wet, so much so that we had to put our coats on the radiators. Some time later one of the receptionists was to come with a telephone message from my brother Bill, telling us to stay where we were as he was coming to collect us. We were both rather puzzled until Bill arrived telling us about flood warnings. When we arrived at our bungalow, we opened the car door to see water from the drains, gushing up, flooding the road that we were on. Ken told Bill that he should get back to his place before it got any worse. We walked through the water until we reached our bungalow. Luckily the water had not reached that far so it was clear around our doorstep.

We were to find out later that my brother Bill and his wife Betty were not so fortunate. Their address was on Anlaby High Road, in the Trinity House Retirement buildings and the floodwaters ran through their bungalow in no time at all. Bill and Betty and all of the other residents had to be rescued from their homes in a boat, through the big gates and out to a safe and dry place. They lost nearly all of their belongings and were given shelter by relatives until a flat was found for them. It was some time before the bungalow become fit for occupation again.

The flood was fast becoming a major disaster and the council came to the rescue of many families. As the waters receded caravans began to appear on the estates until homes were made habitable again. In some cases, flood damage didn't become apparent for many months and so the disruption to many homes dragged on for over a year. This was the case with our daughter

Jenny's house down Patterdale Road but she was able to stay put while repair work was carried out.

During that time, people were rehomed in alternative accommodation, including hotels, B&Bs, caravans for those who didn't wish to leave their homes, were placed in their front gardens as temporary accommodation.

In the days after the flood, many had taken refuge in the upper floor of their houses and one of our Grandson's, Tom, was diverted from his work, as a joiner, to take essential provisions by boat through the streets to those who were stranded.

The floods were a major disaster, as they were around other parts of the country but there has always been a general feeling that the media almost missed reporting the extent of the tragedies in Hull, which included some deaths, as was thought to be the case of the blitz in WW11.

HOLIDAYS

One of the lads said how about getting a tent as he knew someone who had one for sale. Up until now we had mainly used Aunts Emily and Mary's caravan, appropriately named, 'El Mara", on the Marton Road site in Bridlington because we always had dogs and we liked the outdoor life and fresh air.

Thus began camping holidays, first in the Lake District, Dalby Forest and then up to Scotland to the white sands of Morar and Arisaig.

Our holidays together were many in England, on the coach trips and Ken used to say, 'I love to sit back and enjoy the scenery, you can't do that when you are driving.'

Then as the years rolled on, came cheap holidays abroad. We then found ourselves, each year boarding the coach to Spain and later wonderful times to different countries each year, seeing Italy, Croatia, Austria, Turkey and other places and countries, including the beautiful Black Forest.

I'll never forget the surprise on one occasion, when for our Silver Wedding Anniversary, I wanted Ken to visit Germany once again and so I began to save money through the year. That lovely mischievous look on his face when he found out, meant everything. The place that we were bound for was called Titisee, a small town on Lake Titisee in the Black Forest. At the last minute we received a letter telling us that there had been a fire at the hotel where we were going to be staying. My heart sank, and then read on, that we would be placed elsewhere. Luckily when we arrived the damage to the staircase had been repaired, so a good time was had by all.

We have continued to enjoy holidays, on coaches, by car, our own caravans and even a boat moored on the River Ancholme, on the other side of the Humber, which we reached by the ferry, before the Humber Bridge was built.

ANOTHER, FINAL HOUSE MOVE

In the winter of 2011, Jenny approached me with a suggestion the me and Ken move in with her as she was about to put her house up for sale and begin looking for a bungalow.

After six months of searching we struck upon the perfect property which would accommodate all of our needs, especially Ken's in the coming years.

The move to the village of Cherry Burton, just outside Beverley, on the edge of the East Yorkshire Wolds, turned out to be a good one.

Jenny let me have responsibility for turning the garden around, for at that time we saw it as a blank canvas of grass.

When we first took Ken to view the bungalow all he could say was, 'we must have it', then it got to, 'I want it". He certainly was happy about the move. Yes much work was now in progress, with two houses, meaning two lots of contents.

We soon settled down with Ken enjoying sitting in a now colourful garden with Jenny and our dog, Jess, soaking up the sunshine, giving her the odd biscuit.

Throughout the following months, Ken's health continued to suffer with his main illness being C.O.P.D. Eventually carers were helping him with his daily morning washing and dressing, with Ken, as usual, giving them lots of banter, which made a very proud man's dependency more tolerable to him.

Many were the nights that he would call out for help from his daughter Jenny. Despite all of these difficulties he still enjoyed holidays made possible by us having a touring caravan, in which we could take all of his medical equipment with us. He loved sitting on his mobility scooter at Cobble Landing, Filey, where he would buy his crab and kippers, dressing the crab on our return to the caravan in the awning.

Throughout the following months he endured multiple admissions to hospitals. Despite the fact that he was critically ill, at times he still managed to entertain the staff and patients. On one such occasion he was listening to Christmas Carols on his headphones and opened his eyes to the sound of applause from staff, patients and visitors who had been listening to him singing along with the carols.

He was always grateful when son Bill would offer to shave him.

Life was made even easier by the fact that Mark lived close by in Beverley and was always ready to respond on the multiple occasions that his support was called for at any time of day or night.

As his health deteriorated rapidly in a very short time, Jenny was there for him, as always and he died peacefully, at home, with his family. We had taken it in turns to be by his side during this period and I had him to myself during his last moments, after 70 years together, which I knew he would have wanted.

Jenny helped the carers to give him his last wash and I have that towel to this day.

KEN, A MAN WHO WAS DEVOTED TO HIS WIFE AND FAMILY. A QUIET, YET STRONG MAN WITH DEVOTION AND DISCIPLINE. TOGETHER 70 YEARS, NEW YEAR WHEN WE MET AND WHEN WE PARTED.
Passed away 14 January, 2014 at 1.15pm

We now move forward to the year 2017, when our son, Mark was becoming more involved in looking after myself. Jenny put forward a plan, which was to pull down the old garage on our drive and build a log cabin for him and his two dogs, Rufus and Bentley.

The plan was accepted and Mark immediately engaged a firm, with all the measurements and specifications, all he wanted was the shell. Thus began action such as I have never seen, by so few workers. Even our next door neighbour, Suzanne and son and Mark's lads, James and Tom, plus diggers, cement mixers and add wheelbarrows marching passed my windows. Of course me being in charge, to sign for all deliveries of whatever, during the oncoming days, with Mark and Jenny at work. The work began in April with Mark in residence by July.

I can never thank them enough for their attention regarding myself and son Bill for editing my family life stories, which I alone could not have done.

As we move on to 2018, it is August and we are in the middle of a heat wave, the hottest in living memory, not only is Britain suffering as it covers most of the world, with earthquakes, forest fires and other natural catastrophes, everywhere. Temperatures reaching up to 45 degrees and higher.

I am now in my birthday month and yes I have reached my 90th year and I must thank my wonderful family for the effort that they have put into celebrating my special day. Flowers and balloons still fill parts of the house and it doesn't end there, for Jenny is taking us both to Italy to one of the beautiful lakes, in the Autumn by coach.

I will now bring my stories to a close as I must water my very parched garden. But I leave you with one last phrase, "Life is what WE make it"

Joyce Chatwin,

Joyce Chatwin

Me with Jess, Bentley and Rufus

LIFE IS WHAT YOU MAKE IT
Appendix 1

TIMELINE
Characters (family) In Order of Appearance
Baker/Forth/Hodgson side

Mr and Mrs Baker – daughter and son Jane and William Baker

William Snr + wife – daughter and son Eva & Billy (William Snr died on early submarine)

Jane marries Bill Forth – daughter Eva and William Jnr (born with an enlarged heart, died in his teens)

Jane met the widower Walter Tether – (Walt brought with him daughters Emily and Mary)

Jane and Walter – son George and daughter Jennie (Jinnie) (they couldn't marry, as Bill Forth would not agree to divorcing Jane as he regarded her and their children as his 'property')

Jennie Tether marries James Hodgson Snr – daughter Margaret (Joyce) (possibly named after the name Joyce (surname), sons William Lundy & James Walter Jnr

James Snr was one of seven children;

William – (died at the age of 18 in the First World War).

James Lundy (Joyce's Dad) Died, aged 83

Margaret, Ethel, Sarah and Harold + one little girl who died very young

Joyce marries Ken Chatwin– sons Ken Jnr, Billy, Mark and daughter Jenny.

Bill Snr marries Elizabeth Lowery – sons Paul and David

Jim marries Janet Hunter – Daughters Tracy, Kay, son Howard and daughter Sarah

The Chatwin side

Bob King (cockney fisherman who joined the fleet of Hull fishing smacks) marries a Hull girl – daughter Clara

Henry Chatwin marries. – son John Jack William Chatwin

Clara marries John (Jack) William Chatwin - John (died aged 3) Clara Jnr, Jack, Harry, Dorothy, Sidney, Kenneth and Thelma - plus three miscarriages.

Ken, son of John William and Clara Chatwin –

Kenneth James Jnr, William John Chatwin, Mark Stephen Chatwin and Jenny Lynn Chatwin

Joyce Chatwin

Appendix 2

My family

Kenneth Chatwin	born 20/02/1928
	died 14/01/2014
Margaret Joyce Chatwin	born 09/08/1928
Kenneth James Chatwin (son)	born 20/10/1949
Jack Chatwin (grandson)	born 08/05/1991
Brigham Chatwin (grandson)	born 18/04/1994
William John Chatwin (son)	born 10/01/1954
Christina Chatwin (daughter in law)	born 03/09/1951
Melody Rachel Chatwin (granddaughter)	born 25/06/1980
Philip Nickson (partner of Melody)	born 04/05/1971
Isabelle Stella Nickson (Gt granddaughter)	born 29/06/2010
Theo, William Nickson (Gt grandson)	born 06/01/2015
Abigail Rebbeca Chatwin (granddaughter)	born 27/03/1983
Gary Chernowski (partner of Abigail)	born 07/11/1981
Archer Chatwin-Chernowski (Gt grandson)	born 28/07/2019
Liam Ashley Chatwin (grandson)	born 05/12/1985
Paula Palazon (partner of Liam)	born 17/08/1987
Mark Stephen Chatwin (son)	born 17/03/1956
James Chatwin (grandson)	born 23/02/1985
Thomas Chatwin (grandson)	born 14/12/1986
Jenny Lynn Chatwin (daughter)	born 24/04/1963